CIMA's CG[illegible]

Professional Qualification

MANAGEMENT CASE STUDY EXAM

PRACTICE COURSE BOOK

For CIMA's CGMA® Case Study Examinations
From February 2024

BPP LEARNING MEDIA

First edition 2015
Sixth edition 2023

ISBN 9781 0355 1441 0
ISBN (for internal use only) 9781 0355 0815 0
e-ISBN 9781 0355 1458 8

British Library Cataloguing-in-Publication Data
A catalogue record for this book
is available from the British Library

Published by

BPP Learning Media Ltd
BPP House, Aldine Place, 142/144 Uxbridge Road
London W12 8AA

learningmedia.bpp.com

Printed in the United Kingdom

Your learning materials, published by BPP Learning Media Ltd, are printed on paper obtained from traceable, sustainable sources.

IFRS

AICPA & CIMA
Registered Tuition Provider

Contents

Welcome to the Case Study

1 Welcome to the Case Study

How will this Course Book help me?

The primary purpose of this Course Book is to help you to develop specific skills and understanding to meet two of the key challenges in passing the Case Study exam.

Firstly, the next two sections in this Course Book will help you to understand the mechanics of the Case Study exam, and what the examiners are looking for to award a pass. This will set you off in the right direction as you develop the critical skills required in terms of **producing long-form narrative answers** – something very different to what you will have experienced in your Objective Test exams.

Secondly, the rest of this Course Book provides you with a wide range of Practice Tasks that you can use to develop your long-form answer writing skills, whilst also **recapping on the key technical syllabus areas** from each of the professional exams feeding into the Case Study. The key here will be learning how to apply theory in a practical way. Case Study markers are more interested in 'what you can do', rather than 'what do you know'.

The final piece in the preparation jigsaw is to merge all of this with your analysis and understanding of the pre-seen case study for your exam sitting. Being able to apply your exam responses to the case study is vitally important; and you will find this much easier to do if you have excellent technique in structuring long-form answers and a sound recall of the important technical areas in the syllabus. In the Case Study exam you will be expected to provide practical analysis and solutions to practical problems. Demonstration of detailed theoretical knowledge alone will be insufficient to pass.

What role does the Case Study exam play?

It complements the Objective Test exams – having demonstrated your detailed technical competence in the OT exams, the Case Study exam ensures you can put your theoretical understanding to use in a real-world situation.

The Case Study exam challenges you to provide solutions to the type of problems that you would encounter in the workplace for the job role matched to the level of the professional qualification.

It contributes to CIMA's aim of producing competent and confident management accountants – in passing the Case Study exams, you show that you can perform well in real-world situations.

Errata

BPP Learning Media do everything possible to ensure the material is accurate and up to date when sending to print. In the event that any errors are found after the print date, they are uploaded to the following website: www.bpp.com/learningmedia/Errata

What's the Case Study exam format, and how does it differ from the Objective Test exams?

They are very different, and this means you need to prepare in a different way:

Objective Test Exam	Case Study Exam
Per OT exam	Per Level
Computer-based	Computer-based
1.5 hours	3 hours
Auto-marked	Human-marked
On Demand	Quarterly sittings
Immediate results	4–5 week turnaround
All component learning outcomes	High-level themes from each OT exam
Short OTQs	Long-form 'Tasks'
Technical/theoretical focus	Competency/application with a real-world focus

What role will the student play?

In the exam you will be asked to take on a role, and this varies in seniority depending on the level of the qualification.

	Operational	Management	Strategic
Job role	Entry level finance professional	Finance manager	Senior manager
Audience – who you are seeking to influence	Your manager/peers, product owners	CFO, FD, senior business managers – maybe non-financial	Organisational leaders eg Finance Director and board
Common role simulations	Assisting with the preparation of useful and relevant reports using data from the company's information systems. Offering insights that influence decision makers. Making full use of available technologies for collecting, cleansing and analysing data. Assisting in the preparation of financial reports; requiring an understanding of financial reporting and tax regulations. Awareness of your personal responsibilities eg noting ethical conflicts.	Collaborating across the company to make decisions concerning investments, product development and pricing. Using technology to translate long-term strategies into medium-term tactical goals. Involvement in the production of consolidated financial statements. Identifying and resolving ethical issues.	Advising on business strategies to create value. Advising on corporate governance, including the evaluation of the control environment and management of internal audit. Evaluating strategic decisions, including how they are financed. Making the case for digitisation. Considering the impact on the range of stakeholders, whilst upholding high standards of professionalism and ethics.

Pre-seen information

You will be given access to pre-seen case study information at least six weeks before your exam which will allow time for familiarisation with the organisation and industry. You can find student pre-seen information release dates on the CIMA website here: https://www.aicpa-cima.com/resources/landing/exam-timetable

Each case study level has its own pre-seen eg the Strategic case study will showcase a different organisation to the Management and Operational case studies.

Each pre-seen is used for two exam sittings with the November and February exams using the same pre-seen and the May and August exams using the same pre-seen.

What will happen in the Case Study exam?

- You will be given access to the pre-seen case study information at least six weeks before your exam.
- The exam will simulate 3 hours in your role (see above) for the company in the pre-seen.
- You will be presented with Tasks to complete, usually in the form of an email.
  - Operational and Management – 4 x 45-minute tasks
  - Strategic – 3 x 60-minute tasks
- Tasks will usually have more than one sub-task. Where this is the case, an indication of how much time should be spent on planning and writing an answer per sub-task will be given.
- You will be provided with other 'unseen' information as the exam progresses, and you will need to quickly assimilate this with what you already know from the pre-seen.
- You will need to type in your responses to the tasks set, usually in the form of an email response to your line manager.
- Tasks are timed (usually 45–60 minutes each), and you will be automatically moved on to the next Task when the timer counts down to zero.
- You cannot go back to a previous Task when the timer has reached zero.
- You can 'skip' to the next Task whenever you wish, but you do not bank any time – ie your total exam time will now be less than three hours.

What are the key elements of the Case Study exam?

Exam technique	Time management will be very important in the Case Study exam, as will your ability to quickly identify what is being asked for in a task and structuring your answer accordingly.
Exam environment	Becoming familiar with working in the Case Study exam environment will be a great benefit in preparing for the exam.
Core activities	The tasks in the exam, and the syllabus areas they focus on, will give you the opportunity to demonstrate your competence in the core activities relevant to your simulated role in the organisation.
Real pre-seen	You need to understand the real case study sufficiently enough to place yourself in this world in the real exam, and therefore ensure everything you type relates entirely to the case study organisation. You will effectively be working for a different company for three hours in your exam!
Technical knowledge	It is very important to remember that you have already demonstrated your detailed technical competence in passing the Objective Test exams for the individual papers in the level. The Case Study exam will not test you again on the finer details of the technical theory. Instead, it will check that you can demonstrate how a management accountant adds value to a business in very practical terms in the real world.

How is the Case Study exam marked?

The Case Study exam will be marked in the same way as any written exam, eg you will be given appropriate credit for the comments that you make. Broadly speaking if you make a relevant point you will receive a mark. Additional marks may be available for further explanation and analysis.

As a rule of thumb, 'the rule of two' will apply, meaning that each valid point made will be worth a minimum of two marks if correctly made and explained. This may vary between the levels, eg in the Operational exam some comments may attract only one mark, whereas at the Strategic level some comments may attract up to three marks.

As an example, sub-task (a) in the Management Case Study exam may be allocated 60% of the marks, and sub-task (b) the remaining 40%. Each of the four tasks in the Management Case Study exam are allocated 45 minutes (the exam is three hours long).

So we can deduce:

- The two sub-tasks together are worth 25 marks in total
- Sub-task (a) is worth 15 marks, and (b) is worth 10 marks.
- Applying the 'rule of two', a candidate would look to make seven or eight discrete points in sub-task (a) and five in sub-task (b).

Illustration – How should Project X be appraised?

- The project could be appraised using the net present value method [one mark for valid observation].
- The project could be appraised using the net present value method [one mark]. This would involve taking the relevant cash flows of the project and discounted at the risk adjusted cost of capital relevant to the project. [additional mark for explanation].
- The project could be appraised using the net present value method [one mark]. This would involve taking the relevant cash flows of the project and discounting them at the risk adjusted cost of capital relevant to the project [additional mark for explanation]. This would be the most appropriate appraisal method as it would establish the addition to shareholder's wealth from accepting the project and would therefore be consistent with the overall company objective of maximising shareholders' wealth [additional mark for evaluation].

The pass mark for Case Study is a scaled score of 80 out of 150. The scaled score system has been developed by CIMA to account for the potentially uneven difficulty between exam variants, and will operate in the same way that it does for the Objective Test exams.

How can I study effectively for my Case Study exam?

Do

✓ Produce a study plan. The study window for the Case Study exam is pretty condensed, so you need to ensure you have a study plan that works for you.

✓ Try to think in a practical way, eg if a case study task was given to you in the office how would you respond at work?

✓ Absorb any business news you can – anything from new product launches, to acquisitions and change management issues, big share price changes and legal cases. Try to imagine the management accountant's involvement in any of these in the business where it is all happening. Keep an eye out in particular for digital developments.

✓ Practice as many tasks as you can. There are many in this Course Book for you to attempt in your own time. Try and make sure you learn something from every task you attempt.

Do NOT

× Allow yourself to get dragged back into all of the technical detail of the individual syllabus content for each paper in the level. Remember the phrase, 'Show what you can DO, not what you know'.

× Become too obsessed or spend huge amounts of time trying to memorise every last bit of information provided in the real pre-seen case study. Whilst you need to be 'very familiar' with the pre-seen, this is only useful to the extent that it puts your advice into a context. For example, a particular strategy being considered may be inappropriate because of a specific commitment made in the company's CSR statement, found in the pre-seen.

× Try to do everything all at once, or try to remember everything at once from across the whole level. You should just focus on one practice task at a time during your preparations, gradually building up to full mock exams as the real exam draws near.

Preparing to pass

2 Preparing to pass

Exam technique

Overview

Excellent exam technique ensures you maximise your marks in the real exam. It means you score the most marks you can given your level of understanding of the syllabus content by the time you reach the real exam.

The style and format of the Case Study exam means that **your exam technique will be more important than ever**.

What is it about the Case Study exam that makes exam technique so important?

- The Case Study exam assumes you have already demonstrated your competence in terms of technical knowledge, so the focus shifts to showing you can deal with 'finance professional' tasks in a real-world situation.
- All the tasks are timed in the exam, so you simply do not have the option of taking longer to produce your answer than the exam timings allow.
- You are not allowed to return to your previous answers to make any changes once the timer has moved on to the next task.
- Although you can move on to the next task before the timer has counted down to zero, you are not allowed to 'bank' any time you didn't use; you will simply have an exam that lasts less than three hours in total.
- All of your answers have to relate to the case study and be directly applicable to the case study organisation. You have to approach the exam as if you are employed by them, and live in their world.
- You need to ensure you are interpreting the task correctly and doing what is expected by your line manager or whoever is giving you the task to do.
- In order to do all of this really well, planning your answer will be as critical.

So, what does 'excellent Case Study exam technique' consist of?

It can be captured nicely in our TIPS approach:

Time management at task level
Identifying the requirement
Planning your answer in context
Speaking to your audience

We'll now look at these in more detail.

Time management at the task level

The Case Study exam is three hours long, and made up of a number of individually timed tasks. Your challenge is to be able to produce a good quality response to the task set **within the timings for each individual task**. This has been standardised for the 24/25 syllabus.

	Duration of each Task	Total number of Tasks
Strategic Level	60 mins	3
Management Level	45 mins	4
Operational Level	45 mins	4

You will also be given further information at a sub-task level to help with your time management and in the exam will be presented with a table similar to the one below.

Section (task)	Time for section (minutes)	Number of answer screens	Number of sub-tasks	% time to spend on each sub-task
1	45	1	2	(a) 48% (b) 52%
2	45	1	2	(a) 52% (b) 48%
3	45	1	2	(a) 36% (b) 64%
4	45	1	2	(a) 60% (b) 40%

This information will be available for you to access during the exam by clicking on the Pre-seen button.

In your allotted time you need to:

(1) Identify exactly what is required of you.
(2) Efficiently digest the information provided in the task.
(3) Plan your answer.
(4) Produce your answer.

It is vital that for every task/sub-task in the exam you get to the point where you have at least produced a complete response in the time allowed. You need to do so without taking any shortcuts in preceding stages, or else you risk your whole answer diverging from the point and failing to respond to the specific requirements of the task.

You should practise these elements in turn, gradually bringing them together in full task practice, so that you speed up and find you can hit exam timings come the big day.

Identifying the requirement

Unlike the traditional way in which exam questions are presented where the exact requirement is very clearly provided **after** the question/scenario, in case study tasks this will be different.

- Exactly what you need to do may well be spread throughout an email from your manager (eg different 'sub-tasks' flagged up in different paragraphs of the email) as opposed to the traditional approach of them all being in one place with a helpful box around them.
- Spotting sub-tasks should be straightforward, as each will have a mark allocation next it, eg **[sub-task (a) = 55%]**

The word 'and'

The individual requirements in a task may seem pretty straightforward to spot if they are presented to you as a bulleted list or in separate sentences, but even then, you **must** look for the word 'and' within a requirement, as this implies there's more than one thing you need to do and that the marking scheme will reflect this. If you miss what comes after the 'and' you may only be able to score half marks at most.

Where tasks contain the word 'and' it is safe to assume that the marks will be split evenly between these sub-tasks, eg 'Identify the risks and benefits' implies that an equal number of marks will be available for 'risks' and 'benefits'.

Planning your answer in context

Having identified what is required, you now need to plan how you are going to respond.

The **recommended approach** is to do this 'on screen' – ie as if you were typing the outline for an email before running through and adding all the detail in afterwards. This is more time efficient than using the Pearson Vue wipeboard (approximately 10 sides of laminated white paper) and erasable pen provided to you in the exam.

A key part of your planning is to consider how much time you have to do the task and to split this time between any sub-tasks. You will need to decide the key points that you want to make in your response, and how many points to make/how much detail to go into.

When planning you **must** specifically focus on the **situation facing the company in the question**, such that when you produce your answer in full it relates as much as it can to the scenario.

An **important aspect** here is to avoid spending too long producing a very detailed plan that gives you too much to do in the time. Just like in the real world, you will need to limit your communications to the most relevant/important/salient points. Equally, you need to include enough coverage to provide the 'value' that the organisation needs in order to take positive action. This will come with practice and feedback as you prepare for your real exam.

Speaking to your audience

You will be expected to demonstrate that you can tailor the way you communicate when responding to tasks, based on the recipient of your response. CIMA (and employers) want their finance professionals to be able to communicate effectively with the full range of stakeholders in a business.

When you are producing your full answer, the main aspect to consider here is whether the recipient has a financial background. If not, then you should look to provide a more fundamental explanation of any of the relevant techniques or concepts in such a way that will help them to understand your main points better.

Let's now bring this all together in our **recommended approach** for the full Case Study exam.

Case Study exam – the best practical approach

Here's a very practical and efficient 10-step approach to working your way through each task in a full three-hour Case Study exam:

(1) Note how many **minutes you have to complete the task** and the amount of marks this implies the task is worth.

(2) Skip forward (using the 'Next' button) until you reach the screen where the **requirements are given for the task**.

(3) Make sure you **identify them all** and **calculate the split** of time/marks between each sub-task.

(4) Use what you are being asked to do in each sub-task **as a subheading and type it in** to your answer space – this is the structure the marker will be looking for.

(5) Now go back and **read the unseen info** you are provided with as part of the task. Given you know what the requirements are you now know what you are looking for as you read through.

(6) Make sure that you also consider any information in the **pre-seen** that is relevant here.

(7) As you are reading, **insert bullet points beneath your subheadings** of the points that you want to make. As a sensible rule of thumb you should aim for two marks per point, so use this to calculate how many bullets you need beneath each subheading.

(8) When you have populated your onscreen plan in the answer box, you can now return to the first sub-task and start to **turn your points into full sentences**, remembering your role and who the recipient is.

(9) You are working for the real pre-seen company! You must make sure you **relate your answer to the company/industry** as much as possible.

(10) Keep an **eye on the time for the task** as it ticks down. You **must** manage your time within a task to ensure you give a **good response to each sub-task**. If you miss the last one out as you run out of time then you've just missed out on a sizable number of marks of the 100 points available, and potentially a large proportion of those available for an individual competency.

Core activities map

3 Core activities map

	A Evaluate opportunities to add value Syllabus weighting 15–25%	Relevant tasks	Most relevant underlying OT subject/s
1	I can select appropriate capital investment appraisal techniques and apply them in order to support capital investment decisions, including product/service development, digital transformation projects and acquisitions.	Task 1 (a)	P2b (2 and 3)
2	I can identify and use relevant digital data sources to assist in capital investment decisions.	Task 2 (a)	P2b (1)
3	I can explain which pricing strategies are appropriate.	Sample assessment 2 task 2 (b)	P2b (4)
4	I can select and implement suitable business models that will create value for stakeholders, including business models in the context of digital ecosystems.	Task 2 (b)	E2a (1 and 2)
5	I can analyse the impact of disruptive and digital operating business models in the context of digital ecosystems.	Sample assessment 1 task 3 (b)	E2a (3)
6	I can explain the relevance of weighted average cost of capital.	Task 1 (b)	F2a (2)

	B Implement senior management decisions Syllabus weighting 15–25%	Relevant tasks	Most relevant underlying OT subject/s
1	I can apply appropriate project management tools and techniques to effectively manage projects at the appropriate stage in the project life cycle.	Sample assessment 1 task 1 (b) Sample assessment 2 task 4 (b)	E2c (1 and 2)
2	I can identify the key project personnel, explain their responsibilities and set appropriate performance measures.	Sample assessment 1 task 4 (a)	E2c (3)
3	I can select and apply suitable tools and techniques for managing risk and uncertainty in capital projects.	Sample assessment 1 task 1 (a)	E2c (2) & P2d (all)
4	I can select suitable financing sources and explain the characteristics of the different types of funding.	Sample assessment 2 task 4 (a)	F2a (all)
5	I can recognise the characteristics of high performing teams.	Sample assessment 1 task 4 (a)	E2b (3)

	C Manage performance and costs to aid value creation Syllabus weighting 15–25%	Relevant tasks	Most relevant underlying OT subject/s
1	I can advise on the measurement, analysis and reporting on the performance of responsibility centres.	Task 3 (a) and (b) Task 4 (a) and (b) Task 5 (b)	P2c (1 and 2)
2	I can analyse the processes needed to ensure employee engagement, empowerment and alignment to enhance individual and team performance.	Task 5 (a)	E2b (2 and 3)
3	I can compare leadership styles and identify the most appropriate style to use.	Task 6 (a)	E2b (1)
4	I can use appropriate cost management and cost transformation techniques to manage costs and improve profitability.	Task 7 (a) and (b)	P2a (1)
5	I can identify and apply appropriate quality management techniques to enhance value.	Task 8 (a) and (b)	P2a (2)
6	I can identify and apply value management techniques to enhance value.	Sample assessment 2 task 1 (b) Sample assessment 1 task 3 (a)	P2a (3)
7	I can apply the techniques that quantify and present risk to stakeholders.	Sample assessment 2 task 2 (a)	P2d (all)

	D Measure performance Syllabus weighting 15–25%	Relevant tasks	Most relevant underlying OT subject/s
1	I can select and apply suitable tools and techniques for managing risk and uncertainty associated with performance related issues.	Task 9 (a)	P2c (all) and P2d (all)
2	I can select and apply suitable tools and techniques for managing risk and uncertainty in business models.	Task 10 (a) and (b)	P2d (all) and E2a (all)
3	I can use the financial statements to assess and report on financial performance and position, interpreting and reporting on a wide range of ratios.	Task 11 (a)	F2e (1 and 3)

D Measure performance Syllabus weighting 15–25%		Relevant tasks	Most relevant underlying OT subject/s
4	I can support managers by recommending actions to improve financial performance and position and assessing how suggestions impact on the wider organisational ecosystem.	Task 11 (b)	F2e (2 and 3)
5	I can select appropriate accounting treatments and explain their implications for users of the financial statements.	Sample assessment 1 task 2 (a) Sample assessment 2 task 3 (b)	F2b (all) and F2c (all)

E Manage internal and external stakeholders Syllabus weighting 15–25%		Relevant tasks	Most relevant underlying OT subject/s
1	I can explain the financial reporting implications of additions to the group.	Task 6 (b)	F2b (all) and F2c (all)
2	I can explain the behavioural and transfer pricing issues associated with internal trading.	Sample assessment 1 task 4 (b)	P2c (3)
3	I can explain the implications of Integrated Reporting for the reporting entity and its stakeholders.	Sample assessment 1 task 2 (b)	F2d (all)
4	I can advise on the communication process.	Sample assessment 2 task 3 (a)	E2b (3)
5	I can advise on the negotiation process.	Sample assessment 2 task 1 (a) Task 9 (b)	E2b (3)
6	I can advise on conflict management.	Task 12 (a) and (b)	E2b (3)

Abridged pre-seen analysis

4 Abridged pre-seen analysis: Grainger

Overview

Date

You should assume that the date is June 20X6.

Your role

You are a financial manager with Grainger where your primary responsibilities are associated with the management accounting function. You report to Janine Frier, a Senior Financial Manager, and ultimately to the Finance Director, Jacques Maine. Responsibilities include liaising with other functional areas such as treasury, financial reporting, sales, human resources and operations.

Company

- Grainger designs and manufactures mobile phones.
- It is based in Deeland.
- Originally founded about 65 years ago as a manufacturer of consumer electronics (eg radios).
- Product range developed and adapted in response to developments in consumer tastes and trends.
- 30 years ago it became a major manufacturer of mobile phones in addition to other products; 20 years ago it decided to solely specialise in mobile phones.
- Development efforts concentrated on smartphones. Grainger offers a range of 4G smartphones, with a focus on improving its range of 4G phones to exploit opportunities offered by new improved versions of operating systems and new apps.
- Global manufacturer – products available in most countries.
- Quoted on Deeland stock exchange for the last 20 years.
- Grainger does not provide phone services or infrastructure.
- Grainger's **Integrated Report** sets out its vision and mission, which are as follows:
  - **Vision**: 'To be recognised globally as the number one manufacturer of smartphones'.
  - **Mission**: 'To provide high quality products and industry-leading levels of customer service, delivered by experienced and empowered staff. We aim to recognise the needs and desires of our stakeholders in all of our operations'.
- Grainger's **Integrated Report** also highlights the following:
  - **Staff**: Grainger is committed to attracting and retaining the best people. It aims to be an industry-leading employer – has a proud record as an equal opportunities employer, staff receive targeted training, staff are permitted up to five additional days paid leave to dedicate time to charitable causes, offers competitive remuneration (above basic average salaries, profit-related bonus scheme, and other incentives).

- **Shareholders**: Range from individual investors to venture capitalists and large institutional investors. Grainger is committed to building strong, transparent relationships with all investors through regular shareholder meetings, email communications and having a dedicated investor section on the company's corporate website
- **Customers**: Grainger aims to deliver high quality products to customers – staff are thoroughly trained to produce value-adding and defect-free products and to provide exemplary levels of customer service. Customer feedback is captured via customer feedback surveys. Grainger has been one of the top three mobile phone suppliers globally for product quality and customer service for each of the past 10 years. It aims to become the number one supplier every year
- **Suppliers**: Grainger aims to build relationships with suppliers and sees them very much as part of an organisational ecosystem. The need for the reliable supply of quality components is central to Grainger's success. Grainger has invested heavily in a number of joint projects with several suppliers, which have resulted in mutually beneficial outcomes for all parties

Management structure

- Grainger operates a functional organisational structure:

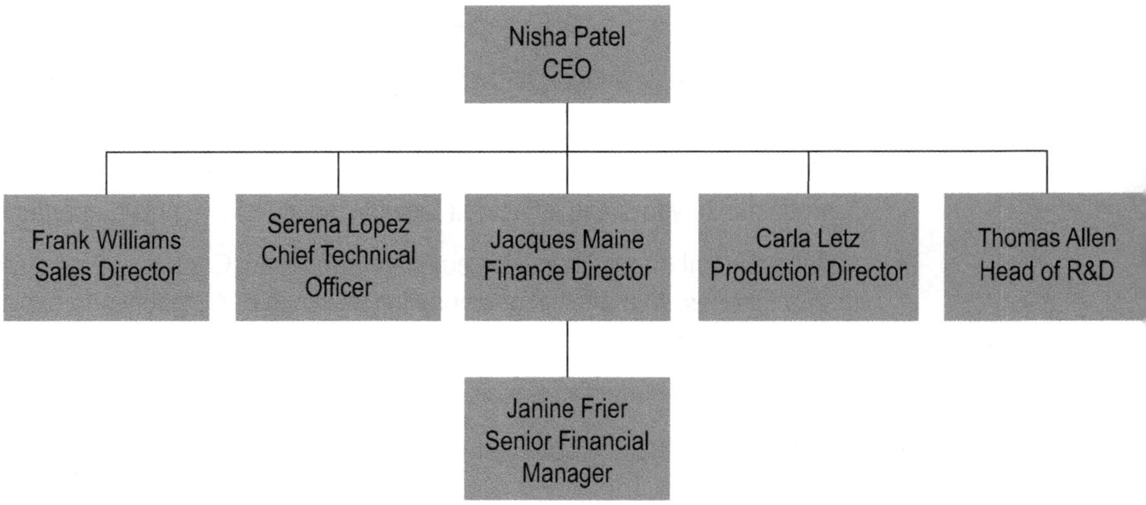

- Approx. annual % increase in number of phones sold:
  - 20X0/20X1: 83%
  - 20X1/20X2: 16%
  - 20X2/20X3: 13%
  - 20X3/20X4: 24%
  - 20X4/20X5: 37%

Deeland

- Developed and industrialised country
- Currency is the D$
- Financial statements are prepared in accordance with IFRS

Industry

Network providers and retailers	Mobile phones require the extensive infrastructure created by network providers to enable phones to make or receive calls from almost any populated area on Earth. The infrastructure is based on relatively low-powered radio base stations that have adjoining or overlapping coverage, so that a phone user is always within range of at least one base station. The base stations can be free standing or mounted on top of buildings.
Contracts between network providers and customers	Most countries have several network providers who compete to sell connections to phone users. Users pay to use these services in two ways: • 'Pay monthly' (usually two-year contracts; payments: direct debits, include heavily discounted phone at 20–25% of its retail value but the cost is recouped in the monthly fee) • 'Pay as you go' (pay in advance by voucher, credit/debit card, bank automated teller machines; phones sold at discount but less generous than monthly contract)
SIM cards	Each mobile phone is identified by a SIM card, which carries unique identifying data. The network provider issues the SIM card to the user. Changing the SIM card changes the identity of the phone, including its phone number. • Manufacturers (eg Grainger) 'lock' phones so that they will only work with a SIM card from a designated network provider • Possible to buy unlocked phones to use with any network provider but more expensive
Phone retailers	Grainger sells phones to retailers rather than directly to phone users, but it has a direct relationship with users who have to register their details on Grainger's website to qualify for the standard manufacturer's warranty, to receive advance information about new models and to access the online support forum. There is also an option to purchase an extended warranty. Network providers often have their own retail channels (shops and online sales) to sell phones and SIM cards carrying the network provider's brand. They sell 'pay monthly' and 'pay as you go' phones, with associated service contracts, that are locked to their own networks. Network providers use their buying power to obtain discounts when they buy phones from manufacturers and they pass much of that discount on to their customers. Mobile phones are also sold by independent retailers on behalf of a variety of network providers. Network providers give the retailers commissions so that the customer pays the same for a 'pay monthly' contract or a 'pay as you go' phone obtained through a retailer or through the network provider.

Functions of phones	The functions of mobile phones have developed over time (chronological order): • Make and receive calls • SMS text messaging • Access internet (Wi-Fi) and email; cameras; music players; handheld games consoles; fashion accessories ('smartphones')
Software	Mobile phones rely on operating systems for the hardware to function. Originally, each manufacturer developed a basic operating system to translate key presses into electronic instructions, such as accepting an incoming call. The current complexity of mobile phones makes it uneconomical to develop separate operating systems. Most manufacturers use an open source operating system subsequently adapted to meet their specific needs: • The operating system's owner grants permission for manufacturers to install software free of charge and adapt it (eg Grainger's logo appears when phone is powered up and the screens that users interact with are designed by Grainger). • Users can then install apps on their device. • Advantages to Grainger of using an open source operating system include: no costs for developing/updating own system, no charge from system's owner, and potential buyers are aware that they can install a wide selection of apps. • Disadvantages to Grainger of using an open source operating system include: most of its competitors use the same operating system so phones have similar appearance.
Radio frequencies and data connections	• Radio communications transmit a signal pitched at a specific frequency which allows it to be captured by a receiver set at the same frequency. • Strict laws exist regarding radio transmissions to avoid interference between signals. Most governments treat radio frequencies as a national resource. • Each generation of mobile has been numbered. Most phones operate as either 3G or 4G. • 3G phones enable basic internet browsing, and receiving and transmitting data files (eg photos). 4G is faster than 3G. • Phones are generally 'backwards compatible' so they can use older networks when required eg a 4G phone that is out of range of a 4G network can connect to any available 3G or 2G network, but at slower speeds. • 5G is the name given to the latest generation of wireless networks. It is still largely a concept, although its goals include: – Faster data speeds (moving from 1Gbps to 10Gbps)

	– Ultra-low latency (time to send a packet of data between phones) (moving from 0.05 of a second to 0.001 of a second) – More 'connected' world ('the internet of things': connectivity built into products and devices, eg domestic appliances, cars, wearable devices) – Grainger studying 5G potential: unlikely to be operational before 20X7
Battery technology	• Mobile phones use rechargeable batteries which deteriorate over time. Battery life is constrained by trends in style meaning that slim phones have less room for batteries. • Rechargeable batteries are problematic as they require a high current, generating a lot of heat, resulting in safety concerns (eg fuel stations: risk of spark igniting fuel tank vapour).

Costing

The cost of manufacturing one of Grainger's most popular models:

	D$	%
Memory	28.56	10
Display screen	57.40	21
Processor	26.60	10
Camera	18.20	7
Wireless section	44.80	16
User interface and sensors	21.00	8
Wireless connectivity	5.88	2
Power management	10.50	4
Battery	5.04	2
Case and buttons	39.20	14
Box contents (charger, earphones, etc)	9.80	4
Total materials	266.98	96
Manufacturing labour and overheads	11.20	4
	278.18	100

Press coverage

- **Mobile Technology Weekly:** The Deeland Government have introduced the Data Privacy and Security Act (DPSA). This builds upon the existing Data Protection Act that has been in place for over 20 years. The DPSA focuses on two key areas: 1. To ensure that data held by an organisation is only used for the purpose agreed with the customer; 2. That data is protected from unlawful access by third parties. Mobile network firm, Access, is under investigation for an alleged major data breach resulting in personal customer data being accessed by a third party. Companies found in breach of the DPSA can be fined D$50 million or 1% of annual revenue (whichever is greater).

- **TECHSPOT, website January 20X6:** Top three developments in mobile tech for the coming year:
  - Flexible phones: Tablet computers that can be folded and used as a mobile phone. Currently in production in Asia for release expected in January 20X7, manufactured by AKIZ Tech.
  - Increased durability and waterproofing: New injection moulding technology is being adapted for use in mobile phone manufacture to guarantee total water resistance. Currently being developed by Mensica Technology and expected to be in production by late 20X6.
  - Convenient Charging Methods: Phone companies are aiming to remove the inconvenience of needing to plug in a phone to charge it. The use of charging ports instead of cables, using built-in wireless charging options, looks set to become standard in newer phone models within the next 12 months.

Key financials

Grainger consolidated statement of profit or loss

For the year ended 31 December	*20X5*	*20X4*
	D$ million	D$ million
Revenue	39,712	34,890
Cost of sales	(22,822)	(20,040)
Gross profit	16,890	14,850
Research and development expenses	(5,755)	(5,688)
Selling and administrative expenses	(6,053)	(5,948)
Operating profit	5,082	3,214
Finance costs	(399)	(262)
Profit before tax	4,683	2,952
Tax	(545)	(343)
Profit for year	4,138	2,609

Grainger consolidated of financial position

As at 31 December	*20X5*	*20X4*
	D$ million	D$ million
Non-current assets		
Goodwill and intangible assets	282	266
Property, plant and equipment	3,820	3,422
	4,102	3,688
Current assets		
Inventories	6,233	5,723
Trade receivables	9,249	8,126
Cash and cash equivalents	10,456	7,412
	25,938	21,261
Total assets	30,040	24,949

As at 31 December	*20X5* D$ million	*20X4* D$ million
Equity		
Equity attributable to owners	20,496	17,096
Non-controlling interests	200	187
	20,696	17,283
Non-current liabilities		
Loans	2,614	1,717
Deferred tax	46	38
	2,660	1,755
Current liabilities		
Trade payables	6,133	5,408
Tax	551	503
	6,684	5,911
Total equity and liabilities	30,040	24,949

Note 1 – segmental information

Revenue

	20X5 D$ million	*20X4* D$ million
Europe	12,708	10,118
Asia	9,531	9,420
America	7,148	6,629
Middle East	4,368	2,791
Other	5,957	5,932
	39,712	34,890

Operating profit

	20X5 D$ million	*20X4* D$ million
Europe	1,830	996
Asia	1,321	868
America	813	579
Middle East	457	321
Other	661	450
	5,082	3,214

Note 2 – intangibles

	Goodwill D$ million	*Development* D$ million	*Patents* D$ million	*Trademarks* D$ million	*Total* D$ million
Cost					
At 31 December 20X4	160	89	78	45	372
Additions	–	30	8	4	42
Disposals	–	–	(11)	(8)	(19)
At 31 December 20X5	160	119	75	41	395
Amortisation					
At 31 December 20X4	–	55	32	19	106
Charge for year	–	11	7	5	23
Disposals	–	–	(9)	(7)	(16)
At 31 December 20X5	–	66	30	17	113
Net book value					
At 31 December 20X5	160	53	45	24	282
At 31 December 20X4	160	34	46	26	266

Note 3 – property, plant and equipment

	Property D$ million	*Plant and equipment* D$ million	*Total* D$ million
Cost			
At 31 December 20X4	1,232	3,901	5,133
Additions	27	722	749
Disposals	–	(267)	(267)
At 31 December 20X5	1,259	4,356	5,615
Amortisation			
At 31 December 20X4	244	1,467	1,711
Charge for year	47	286	333
Disposals	–	(249)	(249)
At 31 December 20X5	291	1,504	1,795
Net book value			
At 31 December 20X5	968	2,852	3,820
At 31 December 20X4	988	2,434	3,422

Financial analysis

		20X5	20X4
Increase in revenue	14%		
Increase in cost of sales	14%		
Increase in R&D expenses	1%		
Increase in selling & admin expenses	2%		
Increase in finance costs	52%		
Increase in profit for the year	59%		
Gross margin		43%	43%
Operating margin		13%	9%
Net margin		10%	7%
Return on capital employed (excluding deferred tax from non-current liabilities)		22%	17%
Non-current asset turnover		9.7	9.5
Current ratio		3.9	3.6
Quick ratio		2.9	2.6
Inventory days		100	104
Receivable days		85	85
Payable days		98	98
Gearing (Debt/Debt + Equity)		11%	9%
Interest cover		12.7	12.3

Segmental information	*% increase in revenue*	*% revenue 20X5*	*% revenue 20X4*	*Operating profit margin 20X5*	*Operating profit margin 20X4*
Europe	26%	32%	29%	14%	10%
Asia	1%	24%	27%	14%	9%
America	8%	18%	19%	11%	9%
Middle East	57%	11%	8%	10%	12%
Other	0%	15%	17%	11%	8%
		100%	100%		

CIMA Sample Assessment 1 – Questions

Management Case Study Question Tutorial – Sample Assessment 1

Task 1

Indicative timing: 45 minutes

It is now November 20X6. Janine Frier asks you to join her in her office. She hands you a summary report:

"We are planning to launch the new Grainger Trams, a new model of smartphone, in February 20X7. As you can see from this summary report (**Exhibit 1**), the launch date is now subject to some doubt.

When the design brief was first written in November 20X5, the Sales Director was keen to sell it as the slimmest metal-bodied mobile phone on the market. The phone was also to have an excellent battery life. The launch date was set for November 20X6, allowing a year to develop new technologies for the manufacture of both the case and the battery. November is also a peak time of year for sales. Since then, we have demonstrated mock-ups of Trams at various exhibitions and trade fairs in order to create a sense of anticipation in the market.

We have not yet broadcast the television adverts that were to precede the actual launch. We can reschedule the broadcasts at relatively little cost provided we make that decision immediately. If we delay the decision then we will have to pay for the advertising even if it is not broadcast.

- I need a report from you on the significant risks associated with committing ourselves to proceeding with the launch in February 20X7.

  [sub-task (a) = 50%]

- I am also keen to learn any lessons that we can from this case. Please give me your views on the errors that we made in managing the project."

  [sub-task (b) = 50%]

Write your report for Janine Frier.

Exhibit 1

Research and Development briefing note on Trams prototype

Executive summary

The two main design features of this new model are the aluminium case and the new battery that should enable a typical user to achieve up to 48 hours of battery life.

We outsourced the design of the aluminium case to Dare Design ('Dare'), an industrial design company with a reputation for creating attractive and innovative products.

We commissioned Dring Chemical ('Dring') to design a battery that could fit this case. Dring has a reputation for making small but powerful batteries.

The internal components and the screen were all designed by staff from Grainger's Research and Development Department, which also undertook the responsibility for overall project management.

The project commenced almost exactly a year ago when Research and Development prepared a design brief.

We did not receive the first batch of working prototypes of the Trams phone until three days ago. Initial tests revealed a serious problem with overheating, with the battery reaching temperatures that could cause serious burns if the phone was in a user's jacket pocket.

None of the tests that we ran during the project caused us any concern. We had early prototypes of the electronics and the screen worked perfectly with battery prototypes while being tested. Dring is now blaming Dare, claiming that the case is slightly too small, which is distorting the battery and causing short circuits. Dare is blaming Grainger's Research and Development Department for using electronic components that generate too much heat for its slim case.

Dring is presently redesigning the battery's plastic skin, making it slightly thinner, and Dare is making the metal used to construct the case a little thinner, so that there is a little more room inside.

Both Dring and Dare claim that they are confident that their designs will be ready to go into production in time to meet the launch date. However, this may be over-optimistic.

Thomas Allen

Head of Research and Development

END OF TASK 1

Task 2

Indicative timing: 45 minutes

Two weeks have passed since you wrote the report for Janine Frier. You receive the following email:

From: Janine Frier, Senior Financial Manager
To: Financial Manager
Subject: Trams

Hi,

I have attached a news report for your information (**Exhibit 1**).

Grainger's Board is getting nervous about the impact that our work to date on the creation of the Trams phone will have on the financial statements for the year ended 31 December 20X6.

We have paid Dring D$75 million for the work that they have undertaken so far on the design of a new battery.

We have paid Dare D$60 million for the design work on the phone's case. We have estimated the cost of the work done to date in our in-house laboratories at D$140 million. That is a total spend of D$275 million.

- I need you to draft a report that recommends the accounting treatment of each element of the work done to date on Trams, identifying any additional information that you will require in order to finalise your recommendation.

  [sub-task (a) = 60%]

- I also need your report to explain how the work done on Trams should be reflected in Grainger's integrated report. Your report should explain which capitals, other than financial, will be affected by this work and indicate the effect on those capitals.

  [sub-task (b) = 40%]

Thanks
Janine

Write your reply to Janine's email.

Exhibit 1

Business Daily

Trams launch in doubt?

Grainger's senior management denied rumours that the launch of their long-awaited Trams phone is in doubt. Rumours have been emerging that battery problems have plagued the design and testing of the world's slimmest metal-bodied mobile phone.

Thomas Allen, Grainger's Head of Research and Development, commented that the new design was ready for launch and that customers would agree that the new design was worth waiting for.

In the meantime, rival manufacturers have been arguing that setting records for the slimmest or lightest phone does little to enhance the usability of new designs. Customers are unlikely to notice that the new Trams is half a millimetre thinner than their current phone.

END OF TASK 2

Task 3

Indicative timing: 45 minutes

You submitted the report requested by Janine that evening. The next day, she asks you to accompany her to a meeting with Thomas Allen.

Thomas Allen, Head of Research and Development	I am disappointed that the modifications to the design will mean that Trams will not have a true 48-hour battery life. We made that a major focal point when we were publicising our new phone. My engineers tell me that they could use a more expensive power management system that would reduce the battery drain and enable us to achieve the 48-hour battery life. I have brought along a costing based on us using the new power management system (Exhibit 1). In order to make a profit from this phone, we need to be able to make it for D$300.00 or less. I am hoping that the two of you will work with my engineers to reduce the total cost to meet that target.
Janine Frier *(turning to you)*	Please draft a paper for Thomas that sets out the challenges associated with his proposed target costing exercise and indicates how his engineers would be expected to contribute to it. **[sub-task (a) = 40%]**
Thomas Allen, Head of Research and Development	Before you both go, I should say that I am disappointed that Grainger's Board is ignoring the fact that the new battery that we are developing for Trams is a truly disruptive technology. If we succeed then Grainger will be able to develop new generations of phones that will run apps and process data constantly, without being constrained by battery life. I would appreciate your help because I am unsure how best to explain the implications of incorporating disruptive technologies into Grainger's business model to the Board.
Janine Frier *(turning to you)*	Your paper should also address Thomas' point about the need to consider disruptive technologies differently from established technologies when evaluating potential new products. **[sub-task (b) = 60%]**

Write the paper requested by Janine (in response to Thomas Allen's concerns).

Exhibit 1

Costing for Trams compared to current model

	Trams	*Current model*
	D$	D$
Memory	28.56	28.56
Display screen	57.40	57.40
Processor	26.60	26.60
Camera	18.20	18.20
Wireless section	44.80	44.80
User interface and sensors	21.00	21.00
Wireless connectivity	5.88	5.88
Power management	21.70	10.50
Battery	16.70	5.04
Case and buttons	52.70	39.20
Box contents (charger, earphones, etc)	9.80	9.80
Total materials	303.34	266.98
Manufacturing labour and overheads	11.70	11.20
Total cost	315.04	278.18

Manufacturing costs are payments made to a third party assembly company.

END OF TASK 3

Task 4

Indicative timing: 45 minutes

It is now February 20X7. The problems that threatened the launch of Trams have been overcome and the new model has just been launched, with record demand for the new phone.

Janine Frier has invited you to join her for coffee:

I take it you have seen the good news about the public's reaction to Trams. This newspaper article (**Exhibit 1**) is very typical of the coverage that we have been receiving. Frankly, we were very lucky. Our Research and Development staff are all engineers. Thomas Allen challenges them to design products that are technically advanced, paying relatively little attention to the problems they might create for Production or Sales.

I need your help with a proposal that I am drafting for Grainger's Board. In my opinion, we should establish a product development team to review ideas for new products. The team would comprise one senior manager from each of Sales, Finance, Production and Research and Development. The new team would seek ideas for new products from across Grainger and would decide which ideas to pursue. It would also review the progress of existing projects, with a view to considering whether they should continue.

Team members will retain their present positions, with some reduction in their duties so that they can devote up to five days per month to product development.

- Please draft a paper that I can incorporate into my proposal that indicates the challenges associated with ensuring that my proposed team will be effective.

  [sub-task (a) = 50%]

- My proposed team will be acting in support of the Research and Development Department. I believe that we will have to charge a realistic transfer price from Sales, Finance and Production to Research and Development and that should be based on the opportunity cost to those departments of seconding a senior manager for five days per month. I need your paper to identify the challenges associated with determining those opportunity costs and suggest how those challenges might be overcome.

  [sub-task (b) = 50%]

Draft the paper requested by Janine Frier.

Exhibit 1

Business Daily

Trams launch exceeds expectations

Many mobile phone shops opened at midnight last night, so that desperate buyers could have the earliest possible opportunity to buy the phone that was first announced two years ago. There were reports of fights between customers who were afraid that their rivals would secure the last phone in the shop before they had theirs.

Social media sites had many first impression reviews, with most commentators agreeing that the phone was even better than had been expected.

As expected, most retailers sold out of their initial allocations within an hour of opening and had to put desperate buyers on the waiting list. Online auction sites did good business, with lucky buyers offering their phones for sale for up to ten times the price that they had paid.

Grainger's share price rose in response to the successful launch.

END OF TASK 4

Thank you for completing the Management Case Study Question Tutorial – Sample Assessment 1.

CIMA Sample Assessment 1 – Suggested Solutions

These answers have been provided by CIMA for information purposes only. The answers created are indicative of a response that could be given by a good candidate. They are not to be considered exhaustive, and other appropriate relevant responses would receive credit.

CIMA will not accept challenges to these answers on the basis of academic judgement.

Task 1

Risks associated with immediate launch

Modifications to the phone do not work

The most immediate risk is that the modifications will not work and that some of the phones will catch fire and injure customers. In everyday use, a phone catching fire could have huge consequences, such as causing a motorist to crash or threating the safety of an aircraft. Given that Grainger is aware of this risk, it will almost certainly be held liable.

Damage to Grainger's reputation

Grainger's reputation will be at risk because it will be perceived as a company that puts profit before the safety of its customers. It will be very difficult to justify the decision to launch the phone without full and thorough testing. Both Dring and Dare will have incentives to make it clear that they were concerned and so the story will be very likely to become public.

Problems arising from the modifications

There could be other problems arising from the modifications. For example, making the case out of thinner materials may make it distort and the phone may fail in the process. Releasing an unreliable product may be almost as damaging to Grainger's commercial interests as releasing a dangerous one.

Timing of launch

There is an upside risk in that a timely launch would capitalise on market interest and consumer expectations. Any delay could lead to consumers losing interest. A delayed launch could also create the impression that there are problems with the phone's reliability.

Project management

Lack of ownership

There has been a lack of proper ownership of this project. It is unacceptable that the external design companies should be claiming to have done their individual jobs properly while the resulting parts do not fit and work together. There should have been a team within Grainger's Research and Development Department taking full responsibility for the whole project, so that the responsibility for the problems with the prototypes remained in-house.

Lack of coordination

Proper ownership would have addressed the lack of coordination between Grainger and the two outside companies. The external design companies should have been submitting samples and models to Grainger and staff there should have been checking that all dimensions were within design tolerances. Then a formal decision could have been taken as to how to rectify any compatibility issues.

Blame environment

The responses by the external companies imply a blame environment. Neither company could quite meet the specifications that had been imposed by the design and both attempted to deal with that by submitting a component that did not quite meet the specification. A more constructive 'no surprises' environment would have encouraged the designers to have approached the main design team at a much earlier stage to report that there were issues. Perhaps the overall design could have been modified slightly to accommodate the design problems with the battery and the case.

Short deadlines

The short deadlines have robbed Grainger of the scope to redesign. That may have been a conscious decision because the products have a short lifecycle and there are commercial and marketing considerations, but there is little opportunity to adapt to the problems. It might have been possible to address partly by setting far stricter criteria for the designers, so that a battery that was even fractionally too large would be deemed unacceptable. That would have meant that Dare and Dring would not have tried to pass off slightly out of spec items at the last minute.

Task 2

Accounting treatment

Definition of development expenditure

The expenditure may be capitalised as development if it meets the criteria set out in IAS 38 *Intangible Assets*. The definition of development involves the application of research findings to the planning or design of new products before the start of production or use. In principle, that definition would encompass the work done on Trams because Grainger is planning to launch the new phone.

Recognition criteria for intangible assets

IAS 38 sets out generic criteria for the recognition of an intangible asset. Grainger will only be permitted to capitalise the costs as intangibles if it is confident that the expenditure will yield future economic benefits. It is also necessary for the cost of the asset to be determined reliably. Grainger's Board will have to consider each element of the D$275 million outlay to date separately. The IAS sets out a further set of criteria that relate specifically to development in order to apply these generic criteria. Failure of any one of those criteria would require the cost to be written off.

D$75 million paid to Dring

The D$75 million paid to Dring appears to have resulted in a viable battery design that uses new technology. If Grainger intends to proceed with the manufacture of Trams then it would be possible to capitalise the D$75 million and amortise it over the product's expected life. It may be possible to modify this treatment if the contract with Dring gives Grainger ownership of the intellectual capital in the new battery design. In that case, it may be possible to amortise it over a longer period if Grainger is confident that it will use the battery on further new products.

D$60 million paid to Dare

The D$60 million paid to Dare for the design work can only be capitalised if the Trams phone will go into production. That would require the technical problems that have affected the prototypes to be resolved and the commercial concerns voiced in the business press to be dismissed by Grainger's Board. If the phone is not expected to go into production then the design work will have little real value in itself and IAS 38 will require that it be written off.

D$140 million spent in-house

The treatment of the D$140 million spent in-house in Grainger's laboratories will also depend on the Board's intentions to proceed with Trams. The R&D costs incurred in-house will also have to be costed accurately. It would, for example, be necessary for the design engineers to have kept records of the time spent on this particular project and for all bought-in materials and components to be traced to the development of Trams.

Integrated report

Intellectual capital

Grainger's intellectual capital will be increased by the development of this new product. The phone has design features, notably a thin case and compatible battery combination, that will give the company an advantage over competitors. The report should explain the form that the intellectual capital takes, including whether it comprises contractual rights, patented products and processes and knowledge that will benefit the entity.

Human capital

The creation of this new phone will also enhance Grainger's human capital by developing skills in the development of new products and in marketing the new technology. The integrated report should explain how the work done to date on Trams has helped the staff employed in the project to develop their understanding of the implementation of Grainger's strategy.

Social and relationship capital

The phone has also enhanced Grainger's social and relationship capital, primarily through the work that it has undertaken with Dring and Dare, through developing the ability to work closely with those companies and through the development of an effective interface between those two key suppliers.

Natural capital

Grainger could also indicate the impact of this new product on natural capital. The intention behind Trams is that it will encourage customers to upgrade their mobile phones, which will lead to the unnecessary consumption of natural capital, such as scarce materials and the emissions associated with their mining and transportation. Hopefully, Grainger will be able to report some mitigation of those harmful effects.

Task 3

Target costing

Significant savings required

We need to make quite a significant saving of D$15.04/315.04 = 5%. There is unlikely to be scope in saving anything on the power management component because we have just negotiated that cost. We may have to find a large number of very small savings in order to get the overall price down.

Many costs the same as previous model

One challenge is that many of the costs appear to be the same as for our previous model. That implies that we have had these costs under review for some time and have been unable to change them. We might be able to have the engineers review those aspects that are under our direct control, such as asking whether there could be any savings in the manufacturing costs.

Investigate big-ticket items

We should investigate the big-ticket items that have pushed the price up, such as the case. Presumably, the cases used on the old model were of an acceptable quality and so we might be able to find a way to make or buy a presentable phone case that costs a little less than D$52.70. The engineers might be asked to assist us in reengineering these parts.

High incremental cost of the new battery

Our engineers may help us to argue that the battery price is excessive because the designers at Dring did not achieve their design brief. The incremental cost of the new battery is a major part of the problem. The slim design forces us to use a bespoke battery, but we may be able to force a better price out of the supplier.

Disruptive technologies

Importance of new technologies for mobile phone manufacturers

Disruptive technologies involve the displacement of established technologies and generally brings about major change in industries. They can have the potential to create a new technology altogether. The fact that Grainger is a major manufacturer of mobile phones could mean that the company is a little too dismissive of the opportunities arising from disruptive technologies, such as the new battery.

Advantage over competitors

It could be argued that the mobile phone industry is one in which the companies that take the lead in implementing and applying disruptive technologies will have an advantage over their competitors. It could be argued that most smartphones offer very similar functions and that there is very little real need for consumers to buy replacement phones. Arguably, a truly disruptive technology would have the capacity to create a desirable new product that could boost demand.

Significance of battery technology

The whole point of a mobile phone is that it can operate wirelessly, powered by its internal batteries. It is well recognised that battery life is a major factor in determining how a phone can be used. If Grainger can develop expertise in a significantly improved battery technology then its mobile phones will have a massive advantage over competitors' products.

Failure to consider long-term advantages

Thomas's concern appears to be that the Board is too heavily focused on making a profit in the short term, without considering the long-term advantages that might follow on from a successful implementation of a new battery technology. It may be that it would be in Grainger's long-term interests to develop this expertise, even if the Trams is not sufficiently profitable as an individual product. Any losses may be more than recouped when future phones use the new technology more effectively.

Scope for developing new generation of apps and services

Thomas's basic argument appears to be that a battery with a higher capacity would do more than simply reduce the frequency with which phones had to be recharged. There would be scope for developing a new generation of apps and services that were constantly on and offering the user data and feedback. For example, the GPS tracking could be left on constantly and would measure factors such as the distance walked each day, the number of hours' sleep and so on. Thus, there would be no need to carry a fitness tracker.

Task 4

Effective team

Significant change to jobs and careers

Belonging to this team will involve a significant change to team members' jobs and possibly their ongoing careers. It will require them to spend roughly one day a week out of their departments, working on product development. That may lead to them being passed over for promotion because they will not be committed to their jobs.

Seek volunteers for team membership

One response to that challenge would be to seek volunteers for team membership. Ideally, team members will be motivated by their interest in product design or be looking for fresh challenges and so would be willing to accept being on a slightly different career trajectory.

Tensions between team members

There is a risk that team members will view themselves as representing their respective departments, which could create tension and lead to unhelpful discussions. This might be a particular problem for the team members from R&D, who may feel defensive about giving other departments oversight of responsibilities that were previously the responsibility of the research and development department.

Need to evaluate team on its results

The most effective response to this would be to ensure that the team is evaluated on the results that it produces, with regular reports to the Board about discussions and progress towards the development of new products. The team's convener could be the representative from R&D and he or she could be required to report directly to the Board on, say, a quarterly basis.

Communication issues

The nature of the team is that team members may struggle to communicate with one another, given that they will have different backgrounds and their interests in new products will be very different. The R&D representative may be the only one to understand the technical issues associated with the development of a new product and the Sales representative may be the only one who understands the marketing issues.

Focus on commercial rather than technical issues

This challenge might be addressed by insisting that communication is informal and focuses on the commercial issues rather than the underlying technical matters. For example, if Finance produces a discounted cash flow analysis, it will be presented and explained in a manner that will be readily understood by colleagues from non-accounting backgrounds.

Opportunity cost

Assess cost at entity rather than department level

It could be argued that the opportunity cost of diverting senior managers will be borne by Grainger overall rather than the individual departments that they represent. If, say, the work done by Sales is less effective because a senior manager has been working on product development rather than marketing then the impact on revenue will affect the entity as a whole rather than the Sales Department.

Measurement issues at department level

It may be difficult to measure the opportunity cost to individual departments because that may be a simple matter of reallocating duties, with more routine work being passed down the department. For example, an assistant might be asked to take over responsibility for the preparation of a routine report and an aspect of the assistant's work passed down to an intern. The cost to the department could be minimal, especially if the team members choose to retain most of their present responsibilities and simply work harder or more efficiently to carry on as before.

Resentment if different charges made by different departments

Any differences between the charges made by different departments could cause resentment and friction between the team members themselves. A manager whose department negotiated a higher transfer price could regard colleagues from other departments as inferior, which could undermine the effectiveness of the team. Even charging the transfers on the basis of, say, a proportion of managers' salaries could be counter-productive because team members could infer some seniority on the basis of their respective salaries.

Benefits from departments' interests being represented in product development

Finally, departments might not suffer any net opportunity cost because they will benefit from having their interests represented in the product development process. For example, Production will be able to identify difficulties in manufacturing potential products and have the designs modified, or even abandoned altogether on the grounds that they would be too difficult to make. The departments could actually benefit from the secondment of those managers and so it may be regarded as illogical that they are being compensated by an internal charge.

CIMA Sample Assessment 2 – Questions

Management Case Study Question Tutorial – Sample Assessment 2

Task 1

Indicative timing: 45 minutes

You receive the following email:

From: Janine Frier, Senior Financial Manager
To: Financial Manager
Subject: New smartphone

Hi,

I have forwarded you an email (**Exhibit 1**) that I received from Serena Lopez, our Chief Technical Officer. Our Board is excited about the possibility of collaborating with Thorp. Thorp is one of the world's largest network providers and their support will help us to promote our new model. There will be a meeting to discuss the possibilities later today and I need you to draft a briefing paper for me that covers the following:

- Firstly, identify the key issues that we will have to negotiate with Thorp, explaining why they matter to both companies.

  [sub-task (a) = 40%]

- Secondly, explain how the proposed agreement with Thorp might enhance Grainger's value chain, and suggest how we might make best use of those enhancements.

  [sub-task (b) = 60%]

Janine

Write your response to Janine.

Exhibit 1

From: Serena Lopez, Chief Technical Officer
To: Senior Management Team
Subject: Rapide Smartphone

Hi,

Just to let you know that our newly-developed Rapide smartphone is about to go into full-scale production. The Rapide will be the first model to use our patented antenna design that improves download speeds by as much as 50% in comparison to conventional antennae. Apart from faster connections, the new antenna improves the clarity of voice calls and reduces power consumption, so the battery lasts longer before requiring a charge. It even permits us to make our phones slightly smaller if we wish.

Our existing range of phones cannot be redesigned to incorporate the new antenna, but we will use it on all future designs. It will offer the same advantages to the 5G phones that we are developing for the future.

Grainger's Board has been approached by Thorp Telecoms ('Thorp'), the network operator. Thorp is keen to help us launch Rapide. If we agree to give them the exclusive rights to sell Rapide for the next 12 months then they will promote our phones heavily through their website and their shops. After the 12-month period has passed then we will be free to sell our phones to competing networks.

This agreement will also give Thorp the right to sell any new phones that we launch in the future on an exclusive basis for 12 months from launch.

At present, Thorp is our largest customer. 30% of our revenue and 35% of our sales by volume of handsets comes from sales to Thorp. We estimate that we presently supply 25% of the phones sold by Thorp, with the remainder coming from our competitors.

Serena

END OF TASK 1

Task 2

Indicative timing: 45 minutes

Two weeks have passed. Grainger and Thorp continue to discuss the possibility of an exclusive distribution arrangement for Grainger's latest phones.

Jacques Maine, Grainger's Finance Director, stops by your desk:

'I have brought you an extract from the minutes of this morning's Board meeting (**Exhibit 1**).

I need your advice on two matters arising from this extract:

- Firstly, explain the business risks arising from this agreement for Grainger and Thorp and explain the implications of these risks to both Grainger and Thorp.

  [sub-task (a) = 40%]

- Secondly, explain whether Grainger should support Thorp's intention to adopt a price-skimming policy for the launch of the Rapide.'

  [sub-task (b) = 60%]

Write your response to Jacques.

Exhibit 1

Extract from the Board minutes

The Board discussed the continuing negotiations with Thorp concerning the exclusive deal to sell Grainger's latest models for a 12-month period from launch.

The Board identified two main areas of concern:

- Firstly, the draft contract grants Thorp exclusive rights to sell Grainger's latest phone, along with any new models, for 12 months. Thorp is, however, permitted to continue to sell other manufacturers' phones. The Board was concerned that the contract creates significant business risk for Grainger and little or no risk for Thorp.
- Secondly, Thorp wishes to adopt a price-skimming approach to the launch of the new phone. Network providers, including Thorp, usually sell new phones for less than cost in order to sign up customers for expensive pay monthly contracts. We have agreed to sell Rapide to Thorp at D$380 per unit. That would normally result in Thorp selling the phones for a maximum of D$250, provided the customer agreed to sign a new mobile phone contract or extend an existing contract by at least two years. Thorp is so confident in demand for the Rapide Smartphone that it plans to sell the phone for D$425 for at least six months from launch.

It was agreed that a further meeting would be convened to discuss these matters.

END OF TASK 2

Task 3

Indicative timing: 45 minutes

Three months later, Janine Frier stops by your workplace.

'I printed a press article for you (**Exhibit 1**). This is clearly a disaster for us.

Thorp sold 6,000,000 Rapides in the first two months after their launch. They received complaints from 8,000 customers, all citing the 'lost signal' fault. We have examined more than 200 of the faulty phones and have identified the problem.

Unfortunately, approximately 5% of the Rapides that we have sold to Thorp suffer from hardware issues that will cause them to fail, if they have not failed already. We were unaware of the problem until we studied the faulty phones that were returned to Thorp. We have written an app that can be downloaded and that will enable the user to run a diagnostic test on their phone's hardware. If the phone passes the test then it will not suffer from the 'lost signal' fault and so we do not believe that they need to return their phones to Thorp. We have released the app as a free download from our website.

Thorp is seeking compensation from us. They wish us to reimburse them in full for the cost of their recall. They are seeking D$2,280 million for the phones that they purchased, even though only 5% are likely to be defective. They are seeking a further D$300 million for the costs incurred in processing refunds, plus D$400 million for the damage to their reputation. That is a total claim of D$2,980 million, which we will dispute. We believe that the recall of all phones is an excessive reaction.

I have asked our lawyers to offer D$114 million, which is the estimated cost of the defective phones, plus D$50 million for the incidental costs that Thorp will incur. If they accept then we will have to pay D$164 million.

Thorp's claim wil not be settled in time for us to incorporate the agreed figure into our published financial statements.

I need your advice on two matters:

- Firstly, what challenges will Grainger face in communicating with the customers who have purchased the Rapide and how should those challenges be overcome?

  [sub-task (a) = 50%]

- Secondly, how should I explain the relevance for the 20X6 financial statements of the figures of D$2,980 million and D$164 million to Grainger's Board and how should we decide on the accounting treatment of Thorp's claim?'

  [sub-task (b) = 50%]

Write your response to Janine.

Exhibit 1

Mobile Technology Weekly

Rapide recalled

Grainger's flagship Rapide Smartphone has been so badly affected by quality problems since it was launched three months ago that Thorp Telecoms, who have exclusive rights to sell the phone, have announced that they will refund unhappy customers who wish to return their phones or replace them with less expensive models.

The phone has an advanced antenna that enables it to download data much faster than any other phone on the market. Unfortunately, the new antenna will only work If the phone is built with the highest possible precision. It appears that the slightest problem with build quality can cause the antenna to fail, with the now infamous 'lost signal' error being displayed on the phone's screen.

Customers should contact their local Thorp shop for advice. The offer of a refund or replacement applies for the duration of the Rapide Smartphone's 12-month warranty, so there is no need to rush.

Thorp has 'suspended' sales of Rapide, although a spokesperson did not entirely rule out the possibility of a relaunch if the quality problems could be addressed.

END OF TASK 3

Task 4

Indicative timing: 45 minutes

A further two months have passed. The Finance Director, Jacques Maine, has called you into his office.

'We have discovered that the problems we encountered with the early production of our Rapide Smartphone were due to inconsistencies in some of the components that we used in production. Many of the components that we buy are generic and can be obtained from a host of suppliers. For example, we buy memory chips from six different manufacturers and the tiny screws that hold our circuit boards in place can come from as many as 11 suppliers. The Rapide is such a precision product that even a tiny imperfection in a part can affect the reliability of the phone.

Until now, we have been unable to identify the supplier of some of the parts that have caused quality problems. Doing so requires a time-consuming dismantling of a defective phone to study the individual components. Even then, some of the items are too small to bear a maker's mark.

We are considering the acquisition of a software product that we could integrate into our manufacturing process. This software would basically track the source and destination of every single component that we buy. Whenever we take a batch of, say, 2 mm screws out of the store and put it into production then the software would record the point at which we started using that batch. When the screws run out then the software will be updated to record the details of the fresh batch. Every single item will be tracked in exactly the same way. If a phone is returned as defective then we can input its serial number and get a precise breakdown of every component that it contained, including manufacturer and batch. If we trace the fault to, say, a defective 2 mm screw then we will know who supplied the component and when it was purchased.

I have attached a schedule (**Exhibit 1**) that shows what the implementation of this software will involve.

I need your advice on the following matters:

- The software will cost us D$500 million. How should we decide whether to fund that investment using debt or equity?

[sub-task (a) = 50%]

- What are the challenges in managing time and resources for this project to ensure that the software delivers the expected benefits and how might those challenges be addressed?'

[sub-task (b) = 50%]

Write your response to Jacques.

Exhibit 1

Project schedule

(1) Reorganise inventory storage to permit tracking
(2) Adapt InvTrack software to integrate with existing systems
(3) Train staff in use of software
(4) Integrate InvTrack software with existing computer assisted manufacturing software
(5) Test operation

END OF TASK 4

Thank you for completing the Management Case Study Question Tutorial – Sample Assessment 2.

CIMA Sample Assessment 2 – Suggested Solutions

These answers have been provided by CIMA for information purposes only. The answers created are indicative of a response that could be given by a good candidate. They are not to be considered exhaustive, and other appropriate relevant responses would receive credit.

CIMA will not accept challenges to these answers on the basis of academic judgement.

Task 1

Key negotiation issues and why they matter

Unit price charged

The unit price charged to Thorp will be a key issue for negotiation because both parties' interests diverge in the sense that the agreed price will have a significant impact on the profit earned by the two companies. Both companies appear to expect a high consumer demand and so even a small adjustment to the price will be significant. Grainger is in a particularly vulnerable position because it cannot sell the new phone to anyone else, which could lead to a major opportunity cost if it sells the phones for too little. Similarly, Thorp may be unable to sell at an attractive retail price if it agrees to pay too much to Grainger. Thus, there is a need to aim for a win-win outcome.

Thorpe's promotion of Rapide

Thorp's management and promotion of Rapide will also be a matter for negotiation and agreement. Grainger will be unable to sell the phone to any other network until a year after Rapide's launch and so it will only profit if Thorp sells Rapide in volume. The two companies will have to negotiate an acceptable compromise over the extent to which Rapide will be promoted. Thorp will wish to retain some flexibility in case consumer demand for Rapide is weaker than expected or another manufacturer develops a competing phone that might be sold in even greater volume or at a higher profit. Grainger must ensure that Thorp aims to maximise sales of Rapide, or at least commits itself to selling Rapide in sufficient quantity to compensate for the agreement to give Thorp exclusive rights.

Length of the contract

The length of the overall contract will have to be agreed, with a further agreement as to when the opportunity for a renegotiation will be inserted. At present, the contract appears to roll over if Grainger launches a new phone within the year after Rapide's launch and it could even apply to new phones developed after that. Grainger may be unwilling to commit itself to giving Thorp exclusivity into the indefinite future because other networks may be prepared to offer a better deal if the launch of Rapide is as successful as hoped. Thorp may not necessarily wish to be tied to any commitments that it has to make to Grainger with regard to any future models that it launches. The two companies should agree to discuss the contract at, say, the end of the first year.

Grainger's relationship with other networks

Grainger's relationship with other networks will have to be part of the agreement. It would appear that Grainger will continue to sell phones other than Rapide to the other networks and could, in theory, sell new models that do not use the patented antenna as well. That could be a source of friction between Grainger and Thorp if, for example, Grainger were to start offering large discounts on its existing models so that other networks could sell them cheaply and in high volume. Or if a new model was developed that did not use the patented antenna but that had some other major selling point. Thorp will not wish to have sales of Rapide undermined by such behaviour and Grainger will not wish to be prevented from earning revenue.

Effect of agreement on value chain

Inbound logistics and operations

The agreement should simplify inbound logistics and operations in terms of manufacturing phones prior to the launch of Rapide. Thorp will be prepared to commit itself to a sizeable initial order in order to ensure that the launch itself is a success and that customer demand is met, at least as far as possible. That should enable Grainger to schedule production in time for the launch, secure in the knowledge that Thorp will place a formal order for that quantity.

Grainger can make best use of that relationship by working as closely as possible with Thorp's marketing department to agree an ongoing production schedule that rolls forward throughout the year after launch. That should enable Grainger to meet anticipated demand without having to disrupt operations or put suppliers under pressure for components and without making too many units and so tying up cash.

Marketing and sales

Thorp will have an incentive to invest heavily in marketing and sales and so might reduce the pressure on Grainger to promote the new phone. Thorp is closer to the retail customers who will actually buy and use the phone and so Thorp will have the expertise to market the phone effectively.

Grainger should work closely with Thorp in order to make best use of the arrangement for marketing purposes. Grainger should aim to articulate its own promotional activities with Thorp's, with a view to maximising the demand for Rapide. It may be possible for the two companies to promote one another for the duration of the exclusivity.

Support activities

Support activities could also be enhanced, particularly in terms of technology development. Thorp will have detailed knowledge of how Rapide is being used and will be able to obtain feedback from customers. Thorp may be able to provide better feedback and suggestions for new product features because of that association and will have a greater incentive to assist Grainger because of the exclusivity agreement.

The best way to exploit this opportunity would be to work with Thorp in seeking feedback on specific changes that Grainger is considering for the future. That would then enable Thorp to seek targeted feedback on potential changes. The value of that feedback would be enhanced by the fact that Thorp has access to customers who already own Grainger's latest product and so can interact with potential future customers for future designs.

Task 2

Business risks for Grainger and Thorp

Grainger loses business of other network providers

The biggest risk facing Grainger is that the other networks may respond to the exclusive deal with Thorp by withdrawing Grainger's other phones from sale through their networks. They may also be reluctant to sell Rapide once the 12 months of exclusivity enjoyed by Thorp has expired. The networks may wish to minimise Thorp's advantage by reducing the exposure enjoyed by Grainger's products. They may also be unwilling to start selling Grainger's latest models a full year after their launch.

Lack of popularity of Rapide

The biggest business risk faced by Thorp is that the Rapide will not be as popular as envisaged. The phone is technically superior to competing products because of the speed of its downloads, but customers might not find that feature sufficiently desirable to buy that phone in large quantities. This market is driven by fashion as much as anything else and so customers may not be attracted by innovations that may be seen to add very little to the overall desirability of a phone.

Different business risks to Grainger and Thorp

The fact that the risks differ could affect the stability of the agreement between Grainger and Thorp. Grainger may be keen to minimise the damage done to its relationship with other networks, who are Thorp's rivals. That could encourage Grainger to spend more on marketing models other than Rapide in order to maintain demand for the phones sold by the other networks, which could damage Thorp's sales of Rapide.

Response to different business risks could be mutually harmful

Thorp, on the other hand, may wish to promote the fact that it was chosen as the launch partner for Rapide by implying that it is Grainger's preferred network in its marketing of the new phone. That could have the effect of increasing any alienation between Grainger and the other networks. Overall, the responses to the differing business risks could prove mutually harmful to Thorp and Grainger.

Should Grainger support Thorp's intention to use price-skimming?

More relevant to Thorp than Grainger

To an extent, it could be argued that Grainger has no direct interest in the retail price charged by Thorp. Thorp is responsible for selling the phones and the retail price is not, at least in theory, relevant to the price charged to Thorp by Grainger. Clearly, though, if the price-skimming leads to overpricing then demand will be reduced to an unacceptable level and Grainger's sales volume will be reduced. The only advantage to Grainger is that the higher retail price will reduce pressure to charge Thorp a lower unit cost for its phones. If Grainger argues for a lower retail price then Thorp may use that as a justification for paying Grainger less.

Possible customer confusion

The mobile phone market is generally associated with networks selling phones at significant discounts in order to attract customers into signing service contracts. Customers are used to getting new phones for no initial payment or a very small charge. A price-skimming approach might be viewed as a change to the business model that might confuse customers. If the initial selling price is set too high then the launch will be a disaster and could undermine consumer confidence in the phone.

Manner of application

The manner in which the price-skimming is applied will be a factor in its success. It may be that Thorp simply intends to sell the phone at a smaller discount than customers are used to, rather than selling Rapide at a traditional retail price that exceeds the price paid to Grainger. If the launch is managed effectively, customers may be willing to accept a smaller discount than they are used to in order to access the benefits of the improved download speeds resulting from the new patented antenna design.

Potential damage to Grainger's credibility

The only other concern is that Grainger's credibility may be harmed if the faster connection speeds offered by Rapide are insufficient to attract sales at the initial price point. In that case, the story will be that Grainger exaggerated the benefits that its new phone would offer and so the company could be viewed as misjudging and misunderstanding its market. That could undermine demand for the phone, even once the selling price is reduced. It could also undermine the credibility of future phone launches.

Task 3

Communicating with customers of Rapide

Challenges

Confusing announcement by Rapide

The first challenge is that the customers have already had a confusing and conflicting announcement from Thorp that it is recalling all Rapide phones. Our position is that only 5% of the phones sold to date are defective, but any comment that we make to that effect will be viewed as self-interested and will lack credibility. Customers will often be heavily reliant on their mobile phones and so they will be very concerned about the possibility that their phones could be defective and might let them down at an inconvenient time.

Press coverage

The second challenge is that this story is likely to be reported widely in the press. That will encourage users whose phones have failed to make posts on social media. Again, that will have the effect of creating the impression that the problem is more widespread than it actually is and that Rapide is a defective product. Stories about customers being affected by a defective product will be far more newsworthy than any responses put forward by the company that sold that product and so it is debateable whether Grainger's responses will attract much attention.

How to overcome the challenges

Encourage customers to download the app

Overcoming the first challenge would be best accomplished by actively encouraging all customers to download the app as soon as possible. If it has not already done so, Grainger should ensure that the app has a clear interface and offers a diagnosis that can be easily read and understood. Ideally, the app should direct the customer to a website or contact telephone number in the event that the phone fails, so that customers can report their problems easily. Grainger should work with Thorp to ensure that affected customers can easily make contact. For example, websites should have sufficient bandwidth and contact centres sufficient lines to enable customers to get through.

Careful management of contact with the media

The second challenge will require careful management of any contact with the media. Grainger should instruct all senior managers to refer all requests for comment to a designated contact, such as a press office on Grainger's marketing department. All managers and staff should be instructed not to make any comments about the problems with the phone unless they are trained and briefed on discussion points. Grainger should accept responsibility for the fault, but should avoid making things worse by offering ill-judged responses.

Relevance of figures and accounting treatment of claim

Relevance of D$2,980 million

The first figure of D$2,980 million is a significant amount, equivalent to 7.5% of 20X5 revenue. It seems highly unlikely that we will ever be required to pay such a large amount. It could be argued that the amount reflects an overreaction by Thorp to the problems with some of the phones and that the potential costs of the returns are largely due to Thorp's negligence rather than the technical problems with Grainger's phones. Nevertheless, we do have the threat of a claim against us for that amount and so IAS 37 *Provisions, Contingent Liabilities and Contingent Assets* would require us to show that as a contingent liability.

Relevance of D$164 million

The D$164 million that we have offered to Thorp is 0.4% of revenue, which is not quite a material sum, but it is a significant amount. It has no particular significance from a financial reporting perspective because we will almost certainly not be making a payment of that amount to Thorp. It has been offered as a counter to Thorp's much larger claim as a part of the ongoing negotiations. The D$164 million will not be reported, but it may suggest that any provision that is made would be for at least that amount.

Discuss the likely outcome with Grainger's lawyers

Our starting point in deciding the accounting treatment should be to discuss the likely outcome of this case with our lawyers. If they can use their understanding of similar cases to estimate the likely cost of settling this claim then we can consider whether that estimate is sufficiently reliable for us to recognise it in the financial statements as a provision. In this context, reliability should be judged from conversation with the lawyers. If they are unwilling to commit themselves to a realistic estimate then we cannot make a provision.

Disclose a contingent liability if no reliable estimate of the amount

If the lawyers are unwilling to commit to a provision then we will have to account for the claim as a contingent liability. The claim would have to be described in a note to the financial statements so that the shareholders were made aware of the possible consequences of the claim. In indicating the financial impact of the claim we would still have to offer a realistic estimate of the upper limit. Hopefully, we will have had some success in our negotiations by the time that we are finalising the financial statements and our note will reflect the amount that is actually being claimed rather than the opening bid of D$2,980 million.

Task 4

Funding investment using debt or equity

Use of cash reserves

The first question we need to consider is whether we need to raise fresh funds for this investment. At the end of the 20X5 financial year, Grainger had a very high cash balance that would be sufficient to enable the software to be purchased. If Grainger took that approach then the cash used would have been funded by a mixture of debt and equity and so that same mixture would apply to the D$500 million. If Grainger can afford to invest using existing cash balances then there will be no issue or transaction costs associated with raising fresh funding and so the overall cost would probably be reduced.

Debt appropriate as low gearing and cheaper than equity

Grainger is funded largely by equity, which means that the company has a very low gearing ratio. That suggests that it would not be a particular concern if the company took out a loan because the gearing ratio would increase from 11% to 13%, both figures being low enough to cause little or no concern. Debt is generally cheaper than equity, so it would make sense to use the cheaper source.

Nature of the asset

The nature of the asset would have some relevance to the funding decision, assuming that fresh finance is to be obtained. The fact that the D$500 million is to be invested in the purchase and installation of software means that lenders are likely to be unwilling to secure a loan against the software itself. The lender will require security, but that will have to be against more suitable assets such as PPE, which may reduce the scope for raising debt in the future.

Cost and inconvenience of issuing shares

It would prove inconvenient and expensive to issue shares for D$500 million, which is a relatively small increase in equity for Grainger. The company would incur significant legal and professional fees to make the issue and the shareholders might be confused as to the reason for seeking additional funding from them.

Challenges of managing time and resources and how to address them

Challenges

Time management

Managing time will be complicated because we will have to decide how the production system is going to be reorganised in order to permit the software to operate properly, with accurate tracking of items of inventory. Paradoxically, it will be the simpler and cheaper items that will require the greatest effort because they will not carry identifying marks or serial numbers. Grainger's production staff will have to learn how the software operates and will have to deliver a plan to bring the factory into line with the needs of the system.

Resourcing

Resources will be a problem because Grainger's managers and staff are likely to be fully occupied as it is with the ongoing operations and so the availability of staff might be an issue. That could be especially true with regard to the IT staff who will be responsible for making any changes to the software that runs the factory as it is. Their time is likely to be scarce.

How to address the challenges

Engage a consultancy firm

One approach to resolving the timing issue would be to engage a consultancy firm that has experience in the implementation of this software. The consultants wouldn't necessarily have direct experience of factories such as Grainger's but they should be capable of making informed estimates despite that. There is, in any case, no specific deadline that creates a sense of urgency for this, other than a desire to put the software to use as quickly as possible.

Create a project team

Realistically, the only way to ensure that there are adequate resources for the implementation of this system would be to create a project team and, ideally, release them from their existing duties. It may be possible to cover for them by seconding staff from other departments where possible and by creating temporary promotions so that more junior staff are given responsibility for the project team members' roles. Failing that, it may be necessary to ask some team members to do their best to cope with the project in addition to their existing duties, but to give priority to the project.

Other tasks – Questions

Task 1

Indicative timing: 45 minutes

You have just arrived in the office to find the following email in your inbox:

From: Nisha Patel, CEO
To: Financial Manager
Subject: Acquisition of TJF

Hi,

As you are aware, our vision is to be recognised globally as the number one manufacturer of smartphones. Although our mobile phones are being sold by retailers in most countries around the world, we do not yet have a presence in the country of Zedland. The currency of Zedland is the Z$ and the current exchange rate is Z$2:D$1. The board believes the most effective way to expand into Zedland would be to acquire a Zedland-based smartphone manufacturer. We have identified a potential acquisition target, TJF.

The shareholders of TJF have indicated that they would be willing to sell 100% of the company for Z$3,000 million. Although we have sufficient cash resources to finance the acquisition from our cash balance, we are keen to use a loan denominated in Z$ to help manage the currency risk we will be exposed to. A Zedlandian bank has indicated in principle that they would provide us with the finance. We now need to do some high-level financial analysis of the proposal. When you were on holiday last week, our new financial analyst did a preliminary NPV calculation (**Exhibit 1**). Janine Frier had a quick look at the calculation over my shoulder this morning, and she mumbled something about the calculations being based on several incorrect assumptions. I am sure that she also used the phrase 'real options' in relation to this proposed investment, but then she dashed off to a financial accounting update seminar and I am left here none the wiser. It does, however, look promising with a positive NPV and the arithmetic does seem to be correct.

Please could you email me notes that set out the uncertainties and errors in the NPV assumptions that you believe underlie the analyst's calculations, and what Janine meant by the real options that might attach to the investment decision?

[sub-task (a) = 50%]

There has also been some discussion about the impact of the acquisition on Grainger's return on capital employed (ROCE) and weighted average cost of capital (WACC). The discount rate that has been used to appraise the investment is Grainger's current cost of capital of 16%.

Can you please explain the impact of the proposed investment on Grainger's ROCE and WACC?

[sub-task (b) = 50%]

Thank you,

Nisha

Write your response to Nisha.

Exhibit 1

NPV of proposed acquisition of TJF

	0	*1*	*2*	*3*	*4*	*5*
	Z$m	Z$m	Z$m	Z$m	Z$m	Z$m
Acquisition price	(3,000)					
Revenue		25,000	25,000	25,000	25,000	25,000
Manufacturing costs		(15,000)	(15,000)	(15,000)	(15,000)	(15,000)
Depreciation		(1,000)	(1,000)	(1,000)	(1,000)	(1,000)
Research and development expenses		(3,625)	(3,625)	(3,625)	(3,625)	(3,625)
Selling and administrative expenses		(3,800)	(3,800)	(3,800)	(3,800)	(3,800)
Interest on loan **(note 1)**		(120)	(120)	(120)	(120)	(120)
Net cash flow	(3,000)	1,455	1,455	1,455	1,455	1,455
Tax @ 10% **(note 2)**		(146)	(146)	(146)	(146)	(146)
Post tax net cash flow in Z$	(3,000)	1,310	1,310	1,310	1,310	1,310
Exhange rate **(note 3)**	2	2	2	2	2	2
Post tax net cash flow in D$	(1,500)	655	655	655	655	655
Discount factor @16% **(note 4)**	1.0	0.862	0.743	0.641	0.552	0.476
PV D$	(1,500)	564	486	420	361	312
NPV D$	**644**					

Notes

1 Interest on loan: New debt finance of Z$3,000 million at an interest rate of 4% will be raised to fund this project.

2 The tax rate in Zedland is 10%.

3 The current exhange rate is 2Z$ to 1D$.

4 Grainger's weighted average cost of capital is 16%.

END OF TASK 1

Task 2

Indicative timing: 45 minutes

You have just arrived in the office to find the following email in your inbox:

From: Janine Frier
To: Financial Manager
Subject: New wireless charging

Hi,

Consumers continue to be frustrated by the limited battery life of their smartphones. Battery life is constrained by trends in style, meaning that we are unable to insert longer lasting batteries into the slim builds of smartphones. We have been researching the use of in-built wireless charging options for some time now and are keen to commence installing them in all our new smartphone models. The wireless charging sensor will be manufactured here at Grainger and inserted into the phone as part of the production process. We need to invest in some new machinery and allocate additional labour time to the manufacturing process to enable us to do this.

While you were on holiday last week, our new financial analyst collected some really helpful data from the business intelligence systems we use at Grainger. I'd like to use some of the data collected by her to commence preparing a net present value analysis of the new investment so that I can present it to the board as part of the funding request. My only concern is that I think some of the data collected by her is not relevant to the investment decision. I've been so busy and haven't had time to go through the data collected in detail but I've attached a copy of her analysis to this email (**Exhibit 1**).

Please could you email me some notes explaining whether the data collected by the financial analyst is relevant (or not) to the decision to manufacture and insert new wireless charging sensors to our smartphones?

[sub-task (a) = 50%]

I am also keen to get your help with another matter. The other day I was talking to Jacques Maine, Grainger's finance director. Jacques mentioned that he had recently attended a business seminar which highlighted how the emergence of ecosystem environments is changing how organisations view the concept of value creation. During our discussion Jacques mentioned that in his opinion, profit is the only value that really matters. I must confess I didn't know what he meant by 'value creation in ecosystem environments'. Nonetheless, Jacques has asked if we could outline how Grainger's strategy of introducing in-built wireless charging sensors will create value for the following groups: users of Grainger's mobile phones, Grainger's phone retailer customers, Grainger's staff, suppliers and shareholders.

Briefly comment on Jacques Maine's assertion that 'profit is the only value that really matters' and explain how Grainger's strategy of introducing in-built wireless charging sensors will create value that can be shared with the stakeholder groups identified by Jacques.

[sub-task (b) = 50%]

Thank you,

Janine

Write your response to Janine.

Exhibit 1

Data collected for new wireless charging sensor

	D$
Investment in new machinery to manufacture new wireless charging sensor.	1,500,000
Specialist component purchased two years ago but never used (the component will not be replaced if it is not used on this project).	300,000
The factory manager will spend four months working on this project. This will be during normal working hours. The deputy factory manager will cover the factory manager's day-to-day tasks in addition to their normal duties. The factory manager is paid an annual fixed salary of D$60,000.	20,000
A technical engineer will have to be taken off other work to work on this project. An external consultant will be paid D$50,000 to complete the engineer's other work.	50,000
New bank borrowings of D$1.5 million at 5% interest will be needed to finance the investment.	75,000
The new machinery will be depreciated over 10 years.	150,000

END OF TASK 2

Task 3

Indicative timing: 45 minutes

You arrive at work to find the following email waiting in your inbox from Nisha Patel:

From: Nisha Patel, Chief Executive Officer
To: Financial Manager
Subject: Balanced scorecard

Good morning,

I was wondering if you could help me? I recently attended a CEO conference where there was an interesting presentation about the balanced scorecard approach to performance measurement. It made me realise that we should introduce the balanced scorecard at Grainger to help us assess our internal performance and processes.

I found a sample of a balanced scorecard online that I think we can use at Grainger (**Exhibit 1**). I want to communicate it to all managers and employees, so that we can start using it as soon as possible throughout the organisation. Let me know what you think. The other CEOs I spoke to at the conference who are already using the balanced scorecard are very positive about the benefits, so I am really encouraged by their experiences.

I spoke to Jacques Maine, Finance Director, about my plans to introduce the balanced scorecard but he has some reservations about it. He thinks that I am going about it all wrong, but I don't know what he means. He did mention that we have sufficient financial measures and that the balanced scorecard might work better for us if we included specific non-financial performance objectives and performance measures for Grainger. Please could you review the balanced scorecard attached (**Exhibit 1**) and:

- Critically assess my proposal to introduce this to Grainger and discuss any problems with the use of this balanced scorecard that I should be aware of.

  [sub-task (a) = 50%]

- Propose three non-financial performance objectives and three non-financial performance measures for Grainger and justify any proposals you give. Please avoid using any measures that are given in the sample balanced scorecard.

  [sub-task (b) = 50%]

Thanks,

Nisha Patel
Chief Executive Officer
Grainger

Write your response to Nisha.

Exhibit 1

Balanced scorecard

Financial perspective	
Goals	*Measures*
Survive	Cash flow
Succeed	Operating income by store
Prosper	Increase market share and increase ROI

Customer perspective	
Goals	*Measures*
New products	Percentage of sales from new products
Preferred supplier	Share of key account purchases Ranking by key accounts
Lowest price	'Cannot buy cheaper elsewhere'

Internal business perspective	
Goals	*Measures*
Technology capability	Manufacturing configuration vs competition
Manufacturing excellence	Cycle time Unit cost Yield
Design productivity	Engineering efficiency

Innovation and learning perspective	
Goals	*Measures*
Manufacturing learning	Process time to maturity
Product focus	Percentage of products that equal 80% sales
Time to market	New product introduction vs competition

END OF TASK 3

Task 4

Indicative timing: 45 minutes

Nisha Patel, Chief Executive Officer, walks into your office:

'Good morning. I was wondering if you could help me out with something? At our board meeting on Monday, Jacques Maine mentioned the possibility of introducing benchmarking at Grainger as a way of improving our processes. It proved very successful where he worked previously.

Please could you send me an email that:

- Defines benchmarking and explains how appropriate internal and external benchmarking are to Grainger; and

[sub-task (a) = 40%]

- Provide examples of how we could apply each type of benchmarking at Grainger.'

[sub-task (b) = 60%]

Write your response to Nisha.

END OF TASK 4

Task 5

Indicative timing: 45 minutes

You have received the following email from Carla Letz:

> **From**: Carla Letz, Production Director
> **To**: Financial Manager
> **Subject:** Performance management
>
> Nisha Patel (Grainger's Chief Executive Officer) is keen to improve Grainger's approach to human resource management so that we are better placed to exploit opportunities in the industry. As you are no doubt already aware Grainger's mission statement makes, reference to having 'experienced and empowered staff'. During the most recent board meeting, Nisha mentioned that she had recently read an interesting article which outlined how empowerment, engagement and alignment can help to improve organisational performance.
>
> Nisha asked the rest of the board to consider how the concepts of empowerment, engagement and alignment could improve Grainger's performance, and to suggest some of the actions that Grainger would need to take to embrace these concepts. I do not have time to look at this due to other commitments and would therefore like you to prepare a briefing note on this matter for me that I can share with the board tomorrow.
>
> **[sub-task (a) = 50%]**
>
> In addition, I also need your help with another matter that I am working on. As you are no doubt aware, my team are currently in the process of putting into production Grainger's latest smartphone – the G-3000 – ahead of its launch later in the year. The G-3000 makes use of cutting-edge mobile phone technology, and features Grainger's latest generation of mobile phone battery, which can hold a charge for a longer period than any other battery on the market.
>
> Jacques Maine, Finance Director, is keen to enhance Grainger's approach to performance measurement and has suggested the possibility of introducing the balanced scorecard. I have volunteered to look at the non-financial aspects of it, as the other board members are so busy with other matters, but I must confess that I know very little about it. Mindful of this please could you prepare a briefing note for me which suggests an objective and a related performance measure for each of the non-financial quadrants of the balanced scorecard that could be used by Grainger.
>
> **[sub-task (b) = 50%]**
>
> Regards,
>
> Carla Letz
> Production Director
> Grainger

Write your response to Carla.

END OF TASK 5

Task 6

Indicative timing: 45 minutes

A couple of weeks later you receive the following email from Jacques Maine:

From: Jacques Maine, Finance Director
To: Financial Manager
Subject: Acquisition of Diand

As you are aware, we recently acquired 100% of the equity shares of Diand, a manufacturer of innovative long-life phone batteries.

Unfortunately, things have not started well. Following the acquisition, Grainger appointed a new management team at Diand. The five members of the new Diand board were all external appointments with extensive experience in the development of long-life mobile phone battery technologies. Last week, respected industry journal *'Mergers and Acquisitions'* ran an article (**Exhibit 1**) highlighting the difficulties that the newly appointed management team have encountered since arriving at Diand. The main issue raised in the article focused on growing staff unrest at Diand as a result of the 'autocratic' leadership style being used by the new board.

This is not the kind of news story that Grainger wants to be associated with and as a result the board of directors would like some suggestions on how to address the issue raised by the article.

Please could you prepare a briefing note which evaluates the appropriateness of Diand's management team adopting an autocratic style of leadership and discusses the implications of using such a style. In addition, please briefly recommend how we could improve the current situation at Diand.

[sub-task (a) = 60%]

The other issue that we need to consider relates to the calculation of goodwill in Diand for inclusion in the Grainger group accounts. The Grainger board has identified assets and liabilities of Diand where they believe that the fair value might not be the same as the carrying amount in Diand's audited statement of financial position. These are listed below:

- Factory premises – these have a carrying amount of D$20 million and a market value of D$25 million but Grainger's board believe them to be only worth D$23 million as there is capacity to relocate Diand's manufacturing facility to the Grainger factory.
- Diand brand name – this is not recognised in Diand's statement of financial position.
- Provision for costs of providing training to Diand's staff on Grainger's organisational policies and procedures – no provision is recognised in Diand's statement of financial position.

In your briefing note, please could you explain whether these assets and liabilities would be recognised in Grainger's group accounts on acquisition of Diand and any issues around their measurement in the goodwill calculation.

[sub-task (b) = 40%]

Kind regards,

Jacques Maine
Finance Director
Grainger

Write your response to Jacques.

Exhibit 1

Trouble at the top?

By Stephen Ford

Diand is a long-established, family-run mobile phone battery manufacturer which was recently taken over by Grainger. Historically relationships between managers and factory workers were very strong. Over the years this led to a contented workforce with a strong sense of loyalty towards the family owners. There was a willingness to do whatever was asked of them if it was seen to be in the best interests of the company. In the past this has been tested when at various times, workers have agreed to take a pay cut, or work longer hours when the survival of the company was threatened. In return workers have always been well cared for, enjoying excellent working conditions and a generous pension on retirement.

The last owner, Aidan Smith, was a particularly charismatic figure who many of the workers knew as a boy during the time when his father was still running the business.

Unexpectedly, Aidan was recently forced to step down due to ill health. As a result, the company was sold to Grainger. The upheaval came at a particularly difficult time for the company which had just won a major export contract that would necessitate a significant increase in output.

Grainger wasted no time in installing its own management team at Diand. The new management style has not been well received and could be regarded as being autocratic. The new managers told workers that there will be changes in how their work is organised and that there would be no room for discussion. One significant change will be the introduction of multi-skilled teams, which will mean changes to individual job roles and the breaking up of well-established teams.

Staff were also told that failure to comply with the new structure would result in disciplinary sanctions being imposed. Workers are unhappy and are highly sceptical about the proposed changes. Production for the export contract is now behind schedule.

END OF TASK 6

TASK 7

Indicative timing: 45 minutes

You arrive early at work and the following message from Jacques Maine is waiting for you.

From: Jacques Maine, Finance Director
To: Financial Manager
Subject: Activity-based management and activity-based costing

Good morning,

We are currently preparing our budget figures for Q1 20X6 and I am keen to take on board some feedback we recently received from Carla Letz, our Production Director.

In our monthly management meeting, Carla voiced that her team can only commit to achieving budgeted margins for 20X6 that are supported by accurate cost data.

I believe that activity-based costing (ABC) might help with providing more accurate cost data as our current approach to allocating manufacturing labour and overheads allocates them according to production volumes. I have attached the cost card for our most popular model of mobile phone to this email (**Exhibit 1**).

I suggested the introduction of ABC to Carla, and she replied saying that there is confusion in her department as to how ABC works; this is a problem if we are going to work with it in the future. I therefore think that staff from the production team would benefit from attending a session that explains the use of ABC at Grainger, including its benefits and limitations.

I would like you to put some notes together which would be suitable for such a presentation.

[sub-task (a) = 60%]

This also got me thinking about a presentation I attended last month given by the CEO of a rival mobile phone manufacturer talking about the adoption of activity-based management (ABM). She promoted the benefits of ABM as it uses the information provided by analysing activities under ABC to help improve overall company performance. When we give the presentation to our production team on ABC, I'd also like to include an explanation of ABM. Can you prepare some additional notes explaining what ABM is and how it could be used by Grainger to improve performance?

[sub-task (b) = 40%]

Thank you,

Jacques

Write your response to Jacques.

Exhibit 1

Cost card for one of Grainger's most popular mobile phones

	D$	*% of total cost*
Memory	28.56	10
Display screen	57.40	21
Processor	26.60	10
Camera	18.20	7
Wireless section	44.80	16
User interface and sensors	21.00	8
Wireless connectivity	5.88	2
Power management	10.50	4
Battery	5.04	2
Case and buttons	39.20	14
Box contents (charger, earphones, etc)	9.80	4
Total materials	**266.98**	
Manufacturing labour and overheads	11.20	4
Total cost	**278.18**	**100**
Margin	43%	
Selling price	**488.04**	

END OF TASK 7

Task 8

Indicative timing: 45 minutes

You arrive at work and are heading towards your desk when Jacques Maine, the Finance Director, stops you and asks if you have a couple of minutes for a quick discussion about some proposed work.

'Thank you for the work you completed on ABC. It is, of course, very encouraging for us to know that the availability and use of data at Grainger could be set to improve. However, using ABC to understand our manufacturing overheads better is only the first step in improving our performance. There are other cost management techniques that Grainger could implement to manage costs and improve performance. My experience on other boards in Deeland has certainly given me plenty of ideas.

As an example, I have been thinking about an initiative to introduce a Just in Time (JIT) system of inventory control, largely because our inventory days are high at 100 days in 20X5, with implications for our working capital management as shown in my notes (**Exhibit 1**). Assuming that the board agrees in principle to implement JIT, it would probably be necessary to appoint a project team to report on what Grainger would need to do to establish such a system.

I am very busy at the moment, preparing a presentation to the Deeland Communications Association annual conference, so could you please provide me with notes that I can give to the board that explain the key features of JIT, and how it could be used at Grainger?

[sub-task (a) = 60%]

I've also been asked by Carla Letz, our Production Director, to explain the concept of Total Quality Management (TQM) to her in more detail. She read an article on TQM which stated that there are four different types of cost associated with quality and that introducing TQM should reduce some costs but increase others. She said the article confused her because she doesn't understand how TQM could be beneficial if it leads to an increase in some costs. Can you please prepare some notes that I can pass on to Carla that explain TQM and its effects upon the costs of quality at Grainger?

[sub-task (b) = 40%]

Write your response to Jacques.

Exhibit 1

Meeting notes – working capital

Year to date 20X5

Inventory has increased from D$5,723 million in 20X4 to D$6,233 million in 20X5.

This represents an increase of 8.2%. Inventory is the most significant element of the working capital cycle. Reducing inventory would enable us to release cash to be used more effectively within the business.

Working capital (days)	20X5
Inventory days	100
Receivable days	85
Payable days	(98)
Working capital cycle (days)	**87**

END OF TASK 8

Task 9

Indicative timing: 45 minutes (excluding background information)

You have just received the following email from Carla Letz:

From: Carla Letz, Production Director
To: Financial Manager
Subject: Component suppliers

As you are no doubt aware, the production team are currently in the process of sourcing components for use in Grainger's newest smartphone, the GR8, which is due to go into production later this year. My team and I have been working on sourcing computer processors which will enable the phone to function. We need to source processors which are small, lightweight and robust enough, but which also have the necessary power to operate the GR8. My team have identified two possible processor suppliers and we now need to decide which one we should use.

The first supplier is Deeland Processors, a well-known supplier based here in Deeland. We have never used them before, but they have a reputation for manufacturing very high-quality components that I am sure will meet Grainger's exacting requirements. They have a strong reputation among their existing customers, both here and abroad, but their components are expensive.

The second option is to go with a manufacturer called P-Tech. They are new to the market in Deeland, having developed their expertise in their home country, Zedland, a market that we are not familiar with and where labour costs are lower than can be achieved by Deeland-based manufacturers. As with Deeland Processors, Grainger has not dealt with P-Tech before. P-Tech represents a much cheaper option and they have indicated that they would be prepared to offer very competitive prices as they are keen to gain market share among mobile phone manufacturers here. Despite P-Tech being able to offer some very attractive terms, we do not know much about their performance record. There is, however, a definite question over the long working hours endured by P-Tech's workers in their factories in Zedland, which have attracted negative publicity in the past. Zedland has experienced significant civil unrest in recent months following the Zedlandian Government's announcement of income tax rate rises.

I need to report back to the board next week on my preferred supplier, but I do have some concerns around the different levels of risk the two suppliers represent. Although we are used to negotiating with suppliers in respect of our existing operations, we must be careful to consider all of the relevant factors in this particular situation.

It would be really useful if you could email your thoughts to me on the following:

Firstly, the specific risks associated with each of the two suppliers.

[sub-task (a) = 50%]

Secondly, the practical considerations that would be involved in negotiating with each of them.

[sub-task (b) = 50%]

Regards,

Carla Letz
Production Director
Grainger

Write your response to Carla.

END OF TASK 9

Task 10

Indicative timing: 45 minutes (excluding background information)

You arrive at work to find Frank Williams, Sales Director, waiting for you at your desk:

> 'Good morning, I hope you are well.
>
> I would like your input on something. As you may be aware, I was, until recently, employed as a Senior Sales and Marketing Manager at Grainger's main competitor, Call-Us. Between 20X4 and 20X5, sales at Call-Us were stagnant, while over the same period Grainger enjoyed a 13.8% increase in sales. I believe that a contributing factor in Call-Us's declining sales was the decision in 20X0 to reduce the size of the sales and marketing department as part of a cost-cutting exercise.
>
> Naturally as a relatively new employee I am keen that Grainger does not make the same mistakes as those made at Call-Us. However, I was surprised to learn that during 20X2 the size of the sales department (which is responsible for all marketing activity) here at Grainger was also drastically reduced, with staff levels in the market research team significantly cut. I am concerned that Nisha Patel has become complacent towards the valuable work the sales department do. Last week I attended a seminar on the role of Big Data and its increasing role in the work of the sales and marketing function.
>
> I am due to give a presentation to the board in a week's time on proposals to set up a dedicated data analytics team within the sales department to support the work we do. I am keen for us to make greater use of data to help improve Grainger's performance. I would like you to come up with some points for inclusion in my presentation to the board. Could you provide me with briefing notes which:
>
> - Explain how the use of Big Data analytics capabilities could help Grainger to improve its performance, and
>
> **[sub-task (a) = 40%]**
>
> - Explain the practical implications that Grainger would need to consider before attempting to capture more data about the end users of its mobile phones.'
>
> **[sub-task (b) = 60%]**

Write your response to Frank.

END OF TASK 10

TASK 11

Indicative timing: 45 minutes

You receive the following email:

From: Janine Frier, Senior Financial Manager
To: Financial Manager
Subject: Analysis of financial performance

The board of directors would like our team to prepare an analysis of the financial performance of Grainger. I have prepared some ratios (**Exhibit 1**) for the years ended 31 December 20X4 and 20X5 but I am too busy to provide a commentary at the moment.

Please could you:

- Firstly, analyse the financial performance of Grainger for the years ended 31 December 20X4 and 20X5 using the ratios I have prepared and provide a preliminary conclusion on your findings.

  [sub-task (a) = 60%]

- Secondly, suggest possible actions to improve the financial performance of Grainger.

  [sub-task (b) = 40%]

Regards,

Janine Frier
Senior Financial Manager
Portafone

Write your response to Janine.

Exhibit 1

Financial ratios for Grainger

	20X5	20X4
Gross profit margin	43%	43%
Operating profit margin	13%	9%
Return on capital employed	22%	17%

Segmental information

	% increase in revenue	% revenue 20X5	% revenue 20X4	Operating profit margin 20X5	Operating profit margin 20X4
Europe	26%	32%	29%	14%	10%
Asia	1%	24%	27%	14%	9%
America	8%	18%	19%	11%	9%
Middle East	57%	11%	8%	10%	12%
Other	0%	15%	17%	11%	8%

END OF TASK 11

Task 12

Indicative timing: 45 minutes

Six months ago, Grainger acquired DGP, a manufacturer of innovative smartphone screens. Grainger had long sought to acquire DGP as it recognised the benefits of gaining access to the company's production and R&D professionals with specialist expertise in the field of smartphone screen manufacturing. Following the acquisition, Grainger managed to integrate DGP's production and R&D teams into its own operations with minimal workers choosing to take redundancy from DGP. All the staff that had previously worked in DGP's other support functions, including its sales and finance teams, were made redundant at the time.

You have just received the following email from Grainger's Production Director, Carla Letz:

From: Carla Letz, Production Director
To: Financial Manager
Subject: Conflict Management

In recent months we have experienced a growing number of issues with some of the workers in the production team that I am responsible for. Unfortunately, the production team has effectively formed into two camps, one consisting of workers that we hired when we acquired DGP and the other consisting of those workers that were employed by Grainger before the acquisition took place. I am sorry to have to report that the group consisting of former DGP workers have become increasingly disruptive to our production operations, and this has resulted in an open conflict between the two groups.

The former DGP workers have become defensive about embracing Grainger's ways of working, with many refusing to follow our existing processes. I overheard a member of this group the other day say that 'working at Grainger is simply not as good as working at DGP. I much preferred it when I used to work for Gary Nicholls'. Just so you are aware, Gary Nicholls was a production manager that decided to take redundancy when we acquired DGP. I am surprised by these comments, especially as we gave all DGP production workers a pay rise when they were integrated into Grainger's existing operations. I suspect part of the reason for this comment is because we amended their employment contracts following the acquisition to bring their working day in line with Grainger's. This resulted in extending this group's working day by one hour a day.

Several managers in the production team have reported that many of the former DGP workers frequently disobey simple instructions and have taken to withholding key pieces of information relevant to Grainger's development of our latest smartphone screen. Only last week three workers in this group were caught during the working day at a local shopping centre, having applied and taken a day's paid leave to undertake some voluntary work at a local charity as part of Grainger's charitable causes programme. Cooperation between the former DGP workers and those already working in Grainger's production team is now almost non-existent and is now bordering on hostile.

When I explained the situation to Frank Williams, Grainger's Sales Director, he advised that such behaviour among the former DGP workers was probably just temporary behaviour following the initial shock of joining Grainger, and as such should be ignored. I am not convinced that this approach would work and would therefore really appreciate your input on the matter.

Please could you prepare a briefing note which:

- Explains how the board at Grainger can manage the conflict involving the former DGP workers that has broken out in the production team.

[sub-task (a) = 60%]

- Discusses the appropriateness of the suggestion put forward by Frank Williams, Grainger's Sales Director, for handling the situation in the production team.

[sub-task (b) = 40%]

Kind regards,

Carla Letz
Production Director
Grainger

Write your response to Carla.

END OF TASK 12

Other tasks – Solutions

TASK 1

Marking scheme	Marks
Sub-task (a): Uncertainties and errors in the NPV assumptions and the use of real options	Up to 2 each

Up to 2 marks per relevant well-explained point which could include:

Uncertainties and errors in NPV assumptions

- Time frame
- Growth and inflation ignored
- Depreciation incorrectly included
- Interest incorrectly included
- Currency movements ignored

Real options

- Explanation
- Abandon
- Wait
- Expand

Maximum for sub-task (a)	**13**
Sub-task (b): Impact of the proposed investment on Grainger's ROCE and WACC	Up to 2 each

Up to 2 marks per relevant well-explained point which could include:

Impact on ROCE

- Increase in capital employed
- Increase in profit
- Decrease in ROCE in the short-term

Impact on WACC

- Financial risk (capital structure)
  - Increased proportion of debt: downwards pull on WACC
  - Increased cost of equity: upwards pull on WACC
- Business risk
  - Increased cost of equity: upwards pull on WACC
- Conclusion

Maximum for sub-task (b)	**12**
MAXIMUM FOR TASK 1	**25**

Suggested solution

Uncertainties and errors in the NPV assumptions and the use of real options

Uncertainties and errors in NPV assumptions

Time frame

The NPV has been prepared for a five-year time frame, but the acquisition of TFJ will probably lead to cash flows being generated beyond that as Grainger will expand into a new market in Zedland and look to establish itself there as a provider of quality smartphones. Limiting the time frame to five years has significantly understated the NPV.

Growth and inflation ignored

Revenue and costs have all been held constant for a period of five years. Revenue and costs will increase with inflation, and this should be incorporated within the NPV. Demand is likely to grow if the research and development departments of Grainger and TFJ work together to continue to improve the functionality and appearance of smartphones and take advantage of the new opportunities that will be provided by the introduction of 5G. If inflation is ignored from the NPV, the cash flows should be discounted at the real cost of capital, not Grainger's WACC which is the nominal cost of capital.

Depreciation incorrectly included

Deprecation of Z$1,000 million has been incorrectly included each year. Depreciation is not a cash flow and is therefore not relevant to decision making; including depreciation each year has understated the NPV. If the tax authorities in Zedland grant tax allowable depreciation on additional investment expenditure, the resulting tax relief should be built into the NPV. The depreciation figure is also too high at Z$1,000 million for five years on an asset that cost Z$3,000 million.

Interest incorrectly included

Interest on the proposed bank loan has been incorrectly included. The interest should not be included as a cash flow, as it should be incorporated within the NPV via the discount factor. The cash flows have been discounted at Grainger's current cost of capital of 16% which will include Grainger's current cost of debt. However, if new debt finance is raised in Zedland at a lower rate of interest than Grainger's current debt, the WACC will reduce and the cash flows (excluding interest) should be discounted at the lower, adjusted WACC.

Currency movements ignored

The NPV has been prepared in Z$ and converted into D$ at a constant rate over the five-year period. The new financial analyst has failed to incorporate the adverse (or favourable) impact of any currency movements between the Z$ and the D$. Grainger's proposal to raise the debt finance in Z$ to fund the acquisition will assist with managing currency risk.

Real options

Explanation

Real options theory is an attempt to incorporate real life uncertainty and flexibility into the capital investment decision. It is argued that traditional methods such as NPV fail to accurately capture the economic value of investments in an environment of widespread uncertainty and change, such as that faced by Grainger in a new overseas market. The real options method applies financial options theory to quantify the value of this flexibility. There are three main classifications of real options: abandon, wait and expand.

Abandon

This can be a valuable option if the investment in Zedland proves unsuccessful; however given the significant upfront investment costs in acquiring TJF, it is unlikely to be exercised by Grainger.

Wait

Rather than acquiring TJF now, Grainger may wish to wait and see if any other smartphone manufacturers in Zedland become available to purchase. However, this will delay Grainger's entry to the Zedland market and hinder its ability to gain a competitive advantage.

Expand

If the acquisition of TFJ in Zedland proves successful, Grainger has the option to expand and acquire further companies there, and in other countries in the future. This could prove a valuable option given that Grainger's products can be purchased in most but not all countries around the world.

Impact of the proposed investment on Grainger's ROCE and WACC

Impact on ROCE

New debt finance of Z$3,000 million (converted to D$1,500 million) will be raised to fund the acquisition of TJF. This new debt finance will result in an immediate increase in capital employed.

In the short-term, there will be a reduction in ROCE as the increase in capital employed will outweigh the increase in profit generated from the acquisition of TJF.

The long-term impact on the ratio will depend on whether the profit generated from expanding overseas is sufficient to offset the proportionate increase in capital employed.

Impact on WACC

WACC is the return required by our existing investors based on the current level of risk they are exposed to. WACC will change if the acquisition exposes these investors to a different level of financial or business risk.

Financial risk (capital structure)

The intention is to raise Z$3,000 million in new debt finance to cover the acquisition price, which will result in an increase in Grainger's gearing and will result in a change to financial risk. Financial risk is in the increased variability in dividends paid out to shareholders caused by the company's requirement to service the interest payments on its debt finance first.

It is proposed that the debt will be borrowed in Z$. This will assist with managing currency risk. The proposed borrowing in Z$ at 4% is at a significantly lower interest rate than Grainger's existing cost of debt which is approximately 15% (D$399m/D$2,614m).

Debt finance is cheaper than equity finance as the risk faced by providers of debt finance is lower than the risk faced by shareholders (interest payments are guaranteed; the debt is often secured, and debtholders rank ahead of shareholders if the company faces financial difficulties). Interest is subject to tax relief which further reduces the cost of debt finance.

Therefore, a combination of the new debt being cheaper than existing debt and increasing the proportion of debt in Grainger's capital structure is likely to have a downwards pull on WACC given their low level of gearing of 11% in 20X5. However, the increase in gearing will increase the amount of financial risk to Grainger's shareholders which will result in a corresponding increase in the cost of equity (as shareholders require a higher return to compensate for the increased risk) which will have an upwards pull on Grainger's WACC.

Business risk

Grainger and TJF are both smartphone manufacturers, therefore, it could be assumed that business risk will remain unchanged. However, Grainger will be exposed to additional currency and operational risks as a result of this being the company's first investment in Zedland. Therefore, it is likely that Grainger's shareholders will require a higher return to compensate for this increased business risk resulting in an increase in WACC.

Conclusion

If the acquisition goes ahead, new debt finance will be introduced to Grainger's capital structure. Funding a greater proportion of Grainger's capital structure with debt finance, which is cheaper than equity finance, should serve to outweigh any proportionate increase in the cost of equity caused by increased gearing and additional overseas risks.

TASK 2

Marking scheme	Marks
Sub-task (a): Explanation of whether the data collected by the financial analysts is relevant (or not) to the decision to manufacture and insert new wireless charging sensors to our smartphones	Up to 2 each
Up to 2 marks per relevant well-explained point which could include: • Relevant costs • New machinery • Specialist component • Factory manager • Technical engineer • Interest on bank borrowings • Depreciation	
Maximum for sub-task (a)	**13**
Sub-task (b): Comment on the Finance Director's assertion and explanation of how Grainger's strategy of introducing in-built wireless charging sensors will create value that can be shared with the stakeholder groups specified	Up to 2 each
Up to 2 marks per relevant, well-explained point which could include: • Value creation is broader than traditional financial value creation (profit or shareholder value) • Ecosystem value creation is about people and meeting their needs • Value creation involves creating value for oneself and others • Users of Grainger's mobile phones • Grainger's phone retailer customers • Grainger's staff • Grainger's suppliers • Grainger's shareholders	
Maximum for sub-task (b)	**12**
MAXIMUM FOR TASK 2	**25**

Suggested solution

Explanation of whether the data collected by the financial analysts is relevant (or not) to the decision to manufacture and insert new wireless charging sensors to our smartphones

Relevant costs

When assessing the financial viability of a capital project, only cash flows that arise as a consequence of the investment should be considered. These are described as relevant cash flows. The costs included in the list prepared by the financial analysis will only be relevant to the NPV analysis if they are:

(a) Future
(b) Incremental
(c) Cash flows

New machinery

The new machinery will be purchased specifically to enable Grainger to manufacture the new wireless charging sensor. This will therefore result in a future incremental cash outflow. The cost of D$1.5 million is a relevant cost and should be included in the NPV analysis.

Specialist component

The specialist component was purchased two years ago but never used. It is therefore a historic or sunk cost and is not deemed to be relevant to the decision. The component will not be replaced if it is not used on this project and the money will not be refunded if Grainger decides not to undertake the project. The historic cost of D$300,000 should therefore not be included in the NPV analysis as it will not result in a future incremental cash outflow.

Factory manager

The factory manager is paid an annual fixed salary of D$60,000. He will be paid this regardless of whether Grainger commence the new investment in wireless charging or not. The factory manager is able to carry out the work during his normal working hours and his deputy will cover his other tasks in addition to their normal duties. Grainger will therefore not incur any additional incremental costs due to the factory manager being involved in this project. The D$20,000 included in the analysis (representing four months of the factory manager's salary) should not be included in the NPV analysis as it is not a relevant cost.

Technical engineer

The technical engineer will have to be taken off other work to work on this project. The company will incur future incremental costs of D$50,000 to complete the engineer's other work. This is therefore a relevant cash flow and should be included in the NPV analysis.

Interest on bank borrowings

Costs relating to the financing of a project (eg interest or dividend payments) are excluded from the NPV analysis as they are already reflected in the cost of capital. The NPV will be discounted at Grainger's costs of capital; the discounting process will therefore incorporate the cost of financing the project. The D$75,000 annual interest expense should therefore not be included in the NPV analysis as a seperate cash flow.

Depreciation

Depreciation is not a cash flow, it is a non-cash accounting adjustment. It is therefore not a relevant cost of the project. The cash flow of D$1.5 million to acquire the machine will be included in the NPV analysis as an initial cash outflow. Depreciation should not be included in addition to this as it would result in the investment cost being double counted.

Comment on the Finance Director's assertion and explanation of how Grainger's strategy of introducing in-built wireless charging sensors will create value that can be shared with the stakeholder groups specified

Value creation in ecosystem environments

Jacques Maine's assertion that 'profit is the only value that really matters' displays a lack of understanding in terms of how value creation works in ecosystem environments. In an ecosystem environment, the concept of value is far broader than traditional financial value creation, which as Jacques has rightly highlighted, has historically been concerned with generating a profit. In relation to ecosystems CIMA highlight that 'value is about people. It is about how their needs are met. It is created by people, with people and for people' (CIMA, 2016: p.9). The process of value creation in ecosystem environments requires ecosystem participants (also referred to as stakeholders) to not only create value for themselves, but to also help create value for others. This is illustrated below in relation to a number of the stakeholders that Grainger creates value for.

Mobile phone users

Mobile phone users are the end consumers of the smartphones produced by Grainger. The development of smartphones with in-built wireless chargers creates value for users of the mobile phones produced by Grainger as they will be able to purchase devices that provide better battery life. To date, mobile phone users have been frustrated by the limited battery life offered by their smartphone which has been caused by the slim build of the device. Grainger's new strategy overcomes this issue and means that the company will be better placed to attract users to purchase one of its devices again in the future.

Phone retailers

Phone retailers represent Grainger's customers. The success of phone retailers will be driven by selling smartphones which mobile phone users want to purchase. As highlighted above this means having devices that feature the latest technologies such as in-built wireless chargers. To ensure that the process of value creation for Grainger's customers is not hampered when its new smartphones are launched, the company will need to ensure that it has sufficient levels of inventory to meet demand, and to ensure that the customer service elements needed to handle any queries with the new devices are in place. These aspects create value for the phone retailers.

Staff

The introduction of the wireless charging sensor system helps to support Grainger's approach to human resource management. As Grainger aims to be a leading employer, developing smartphones with cutting-edge technology creates value for the workers involved as they benefit from being a part of an industry-leading project. Such involvement helps workers to develop their skills and enhances their future career prospects. Grainger's employees also benefit as such projects enhance their prospects of remaining in employment.

Suppliers

The introduction of the in-built wireless chargers in Grainger's smartphones creates value for suppliers as it increases the scope for them to sell more components to Grainger for use in manufacturing devices. Value is also created as suppliers – who have historically worked with the company to complete a number of joint projects – may be able to forge even closer ties with Grainger, thereby enhancing the goodwill that exists. Many of these have resulted in mutually beneficial outcomes for both parties. Therefore, the new technology may provide suppliers with insights which they can deploy in the development of the components that they provide to Grainger in the future.

Shareholders

Provided Grainger can sell the in-built wireless sensor smartphones at a profit, this will create value for Grainger's shareholders in the form of improved dividends. Non-monetary value will also be created for shareholders as the decision to develop the new technology will provide shareholders with reassurance over the security of their investment and enhance the prospects of them maintaining their investment in the future.

TASK 3

Marking scheme	Marks
Sub-task (a): Balanced scorecard critical assessment	Up to 2 each
Up to 2 marks per relevant well-explained point which could include:	
• Top down control	
• Measures must be specific to Grainger	
• Implementing and reviewing	
• Conflicting measures	
• Too many measures	
• Management commitment	
Maximum for sub-task (a)	**12**
Sub-task (b): Possible performance objectives and measures	Up to 2 each
Up to 2 marks per relevant well-explained point which could include:	
Innovation and learning perspective	
• Objective: Training and development	
• Measure: Number of days of training per employee per year	
Internal business perspective	
• Objective: Minimise material wastage during manufacturing process	
• Measure: Percentage of purchased materials utilised in production	
Customer perspective	
• Objective: Customer satisfaction	
• Measure: Number of returned products	
Maximum for sub-task (b)	**13**
MAXIMUM FOR TASK 3	**25**

Tutorial note: You will earn marks for **relevant** points even if they are different from the ones we have included in the suggested solution.

Suggested solution

Balanced scorecard critical assessment

Top down control

The balanced scorecard should not be used to exert top down control. In order to be effective, target setting should be a collaborative process. Targets should be based on information from those that are most familiar with a department or process. For example, Frank Williams (Sales Director), should be actively involved in selecting customer perspective measures.

The chosen measures in the sample scorecard may not be suitable. As an example, 'operating income by store' would not apply to Grainger's business model.

I would strongly recommend that input from other members of the senior team be sought. Thomas Allen (Head of R&D) should have a lot of useful and relevant input when setting the innovation and learning goals.

Measures must be specific to Grainger

The sample balanced scorecard that you attached is not designed for Grainger or aligned to its strategy, and therefore I question the value of some of the selected measures. The sample you have provided has a customer goal of 'lowest price', measured via 'cannot buy cheaper elsewhere'. I have concerns about this performance measure. Although our principal customers, the network providers, do tend to seek bulk buy discounts, they will not select the devices solely based on price as they will need to meet the technological and design requirements of the end-users. Our mission is to 'provide high quality products and industry leading levels of customer service' and Grainger has been one of the top three mobile phone suppliers globally for product quality and customer service for each of the past 10 years. Therefore, the end-users of Grainger's mobiles will be more concerned with quality than price. Some will upgrade their phones to take advantage of enhanced functionality whilst others see their phones as fashion accessories and will upgrade to stay abreast of current trends.

For this to be specific to Grainger, we need to focus upon how the company continues to make its products attractive to end-users, particularly when the same operating system is used by our competitors and there is little to distinguish between our phones and theirs. We must use our strong market position to remain ahead. Research and Development expenditure is critical to the success of Grainger, a more specific financial measure could be to improve the return on development expenditure.

Implementing and reviewing

The board of Grainger should agree on an appropriate time frame for the implementation of the balanced scorecard and consider any cultural issues that may arise. Once implemented, measures should be regularly reviewed to make sure they remain relevant in a changing market. The industry moves rapidly and with the exploration of 5G technology already starting, it is important that measures are regularly reviewed to remain relevant.

Conflicting measures

There are some measures in the scorecard that may naturally conflict, and it is often difficult to determine the balance which will achieve the best results. For example, Grainger will be investing in 5G, and this will result in an increase in R&D costs, which may conflict with financial measures such as increasing cash flow. Because of potential conflicts it is important for Grainger to identify relationships between perspectives, as it will allow appropriate prioritisation and implementation of strategies.

Too many measures

Not only do appropriate specific measures have to be devised, but the number of measures must be agreed. Too many measures will result in 'information overload' and there is a concern that these targets become the overriding goal to the detriment of our primary goal of maximising the returns to shareholders (a key stakeholder as we are a listed company). When selecting measures, it is important to measure things that add value to Grainger, not just those that are easy to measure.

When evaluating our internal business processes, we could look at the release time for new products. Grainger should identify where delays are likely to occur and look at ways to alleviate them. However, any reduction in development and production time should not be achieved at the expense of quality.

Management commitment

The balanced scorecard can only be effective if senior managers commit to it. If they revert to focusing solely on the financial measures they are used to, then the value of introducing additional measures will be reduced. Jacques Maine has already raised concerns about its implementation. Firstly, Nisha Patel as CEO needs to convince the board of the merits of introducing the balanced scorecard. A lot of time will then be invested by the board when setting appropriate measures. The next step will be to hold workshops to communicate the advantages of the balanced scorecard across the organisation.

Possible performance objectives and measures

Innovation and learning perspective

Performance objective

The dynamic nature of the mobile phone industry means that we must constantly innovate to ensure Grainger remains competitive. This requires insight to be able to anticipate and meet the demands of the end-user as well as ensuring our product's specification and features keep pace with those of our competitors. This means we should make training and development of our design engineers a performance objective for Grainger.

Performance measure

An appropriate measure to assess Grainger's ability to develop the skills of our design engineers could be the number of days' training each engineer receives over the course of a year. This should help Grainger to exploit opportunities offered by new, improved versions of operating systems and apps. It should also enable Grainger to keep abreast of the upcoming 5G technology and to incorporate the latest features required by end-users such as those mentioned in the January 20X6 Techspot article (flexible phones, increased durability and waterproofing and convenient charging methods).

Internal business perspective

Performance objective

As a manufacturer of mobile phones, we need to ensure that our production process is as efficient as possible in order to maximise our margins. This is particularly important as Grainger is a quoted company with shareholders that include large institutional investors who will want to maximise the return on their investment. Therefore, a suitable performance objective would be to minimise wastage of raw material components in our production process.

Performance measure

At Grainger, an appropriate measure could be the percentage of raw materials purchased that are subsequently utilised in the production process when manufacturing smartphones. Grainger should aim to keep this percentage as high as possible with the aim of minimising the loss of components through human or machine error during the manufacturing process.

Customer perspective

Performance objective

Although Grainger has a well-recognised brand, brand loyalty among our customers is not guaranteed. Network providers and independent retailers will only stock our phones if they are demanded by the end-user. This should be the case if end-users are pleased with the product and have had a trouble-free experience with them. The network providers and independent retailers may reduce the size of their purchases from Grainger if they start to receive a high volume of complaints from end-users about our products and/or receive large numbers of phones returned. Therefore, an appropriate objective should focus on the need to maintain and improve on customer satisfaction.

Performance measure

An appropriate measure would be to measure the number of faulty phones returned to us by network providers and independent retailers (our customers) in a period (ie week or month). A short measurement period is recommended to allow us to take corrective action immediately following a problem becoming apparent. This is especially important in the short-term after each time a new version of our phone is released as it is likely that during this time most issues will be raised.

Tutorial note: For clarity, please note that Grainger's customers and the end-users of the phones are not the same. Grainger's customers are the network providers and independent retailers. These network providers and independent retailers then sell the handset (and associated contract with texts, data and minutes of calls) to the end-users. Ultimately, although we do not sell phones directly to the end-user, demand from our customers (network providers and independent retailers) will be driven by demand from end-users.

TASK 4

Marking scheme	**Marks**
Sub-task (a): Definition of benchmarking and appropriateness to Grainger	Up to 2 each

Up to 2 marks per relevant well-explained point which could include:

- Definition of benchmarking
- Explanation of internal benchmarking
- Appropriateness of internal benchmarking:
  - In-house performance data likely to exist
  - Problems with comparing different internal business areas
  - Appropriate to use within separate business areas
- Explanation of external benchmarking
- Appropriateness of external benchmarking:
  - Difficulty of obtaining internal information on competitors
  - Appropriate to use with publicly available data

Maximum for sub-task (a)	**10**
Sub-task (b): Examples of how to apply each type of benchmarking at Grainger	Up to 2 each

Up to 2 marks per relevant well-explained point which could include:

Internal benchmarking:

- Production efficiencies of different production teams
- Warehouse and shipping from different sites
- Customer surveys for different products
- Performance of different subsidiaries

External benchmarking:

- Published financial statements
- Market price of competitors' products
- Phone features
- Industry averages
- Social media

Maximum for sub-task (b)	**15**
MAXIMUM FOR TASK 4	**25**

Tutorial note: For the appropriateness of benchmarking to Grainger in sub-task (a) and the examples in sub-task (b), you will earn marks for **relevant** points even if they are different from the ones we have included in the suggested solution.

Suggested solution

Definition of benchmarking and appropriateness to Grainger

Definition of benchmarking

Benchmarking would involve Grainger comparing its performance with the best available performance by a relevant comparator or the performance of an organisation regarded as following best practice in its operations. If Grainger's performance is below this benchmark, then it should look at finding ways of reducing the gap between current performance and the benchmark.

Internal benchmarking

Explanation

Internal benchmarking is a method of comparing one operating unit or business function with another within the same organisation.

Appropriateness to Grainger

It should be relatively straightforward to introduce since it is likely that in-house performance data already exists. However, we need to make sure the activities are comparable for the benchmarking exercise to be effective.

At Grainger, we have the following business functions:

- Sales
- Technical
- Finance
- Production
- Research and development.

Each of our business functions inevitably operates differently. This reduces the appropriateness of internal benchmarking between each activity, as they simply won't have similar enough processes to allow a valid comparison to be made.

However, benchmarking within each of the business functions is likely to be appropriate here. Internal benchmarking however, is unlikely to lead to being the best in the industry.

External benchmarking

Explanation

External benchmarking is where information is gathered about other companies. Where these companies are direct competitors it is known as 'competitive benchmarking'. For Grainger, this would involve comparison to other mobile phone manufacturers in Deeland.

Where the companies are non-competing businesses with similar processes (for example, Deeland manufacturers of other electronic products), this is referred to as functional benchmarking.

If the comparator is industry average performance data (for example, the mobile phone manufacturing industry data in Deeland), this is referred to as 'strategic benchmarking'.

Appropriateness

External benchmarking is likely to be more difficult to perform than internal benchmarking. Our competitors are unlikely to willingly provide any internal information (such as management accounts or product designs) for comparison.

However, by using publicly available information, it is possible to observe performance of other companies and compare the performance of their products against our own. Therefore, it is appropriate for use at Grainger.

Examples of how to apply each type of benchmarking at Grainger

Internal benchmarking

Production efficiencies of different production teams

Grainger could monitor production efficiencies of each production team to identify the best performing team. The standard of the highest performing production team could then become the target level for all teams with the aim of improving productivity.

Warehouse and shipping from different sites

Grainger could monitor warehouse and shipping data (of mobile phones to retailers) of its different sites across Deeland. The standard of the higher performing site could then become the target level for all sites with the aim of minimising warehousing costs and shipping costs and time to customers.

Customer surveys for different products

Grainger could compare data from its customer surveys for the different types of mobile phones it sells. The customer satisfaction level for its most successful product could then become the target level for all products.

Performance of different subsidiaries

The fact that Grainger prepares consolidated financial statements and the presence of goodwill in its group statement of financial position indicate that Grainger has subsidiaries. The performance of each of its subsidiaries could be compared with the highest performing subsidiary setting the target level.

External benchmarking

Published financial statements

Comparisons can be made between published financial statements. For example, we could compare our research and development expenses to our nearest competitor in the mobile phone manufacturing market in Deeland. This will enable us to assess whether we need to increase spending in this area to ensure our future products remain competitive and provide end-users with the latest features. However, to get the full picture, we would also need to review the notes to the accounts for the competitor so we can compare the amount of development costs capitalised and amortised in the year. Different accounting policies adopted by competitors could lead to such comparisons being meaningless.

Market price of competitors' products

We can compare the market price of our phones with our nearest competitors' offerings, ensuring that we maximise comparability by selecting another provider of high-quality smartphones in Deeland. If the price at which our competitors' phones are sold to the end-user are lower than ours, it is likely that they have offered the retailers a lower price than we do. If this is the case, it might indicate that we need to consider reducing our prices to help boost demand for our products. Further, investigation would, however, be required before a final decision to cut prices is made.

Phone features

Our engineers can obtain versions of our competitors' products and reverse engineer them. Reverse engineering would involve taking apart one of our competitor's phones in order to see how it works. This is a highly specialised skill but may allow us to discover weaknesses in the product or improvements that we could make in our own phones.

Industry averages

It is likely that the Deeland Government gathers statistics on the mobile phone industry in Deeland by collating an external database of industry average performance data. We can compare Grainger data against these industry averages to identify potential areas for improvement. This is an example of strategic benchmarking.

Social media

Customers typically post feedback on products on social media. This can include ratings of particular products. Grainger could compare its average customer rating by product to its direct competitors in the mobile phone industry in Deeland.

TASK 5

Marking scheme	Marks
Sub-task (a): Empowerment, engagement and alignment in improving performance	Up to 2 each
Up to 2 marks per relevant well-explained point which could include:	
Empowerment	
• Gives staff greater freedom	
• Staff can identify improvements to internal processes	
• Permits employee-led schemes	
• Requires management to change their mindset	
Engagement	
• Empowerment only works if staff are engaged	
• Establish talent management programmes	
• Set realistic targets and allow involvement	
• Develop a suitable culture and management style	
Alignment	
• Vertical	
• Horizontal	
Maximum for sub task (a)	**13**
Sub-task (b): Balanced scorecard	
Up to 2 marks per relevant well-explained point which could include:	Up to 2 each
Customer perspective	
• Objective	
• Performance measure	
Innovation and learning perspective	
• Objective	
• Performance measure	
Internal business perspective	
• Objective	
• Performance measure	
Maximum for sub-task (b)	**12**
MAXIMUM FOR TASK 5	**25**

Suggested solution

Tutorial note: You will earn marks for relevant points even if they are different from the ones we have included in the suggested solution.

The solution to sub-task (a) is longer than you would be expected to produce under exam conditions. It is provided here to aid your learning.

Empowerment, engagement and alignment to improve performance

Empowerment

Empowerment refers to making workers responsible for achieving, and setting work targets, while providing freedom to make decisions about how to they are to be achieved. Empowerment is often associated with the development of new technology. As such this would be highly appropriate for Grainger as the company needs to actively develop the latest smartphones so that they remain appealing to end users. Failure to produce smartphones that people want heightens the risk that they purchase their devices from rival firms.

Grainger is currently one of the top three mobile phone suppliers in the world for product quality, however it has set itself the aim of becoming the number one supplier. A programme of empowerment would enable Grainger to make better use of its staff and build upon the fact that its workers are already recognised as being highly trained in adding value and manufacturing defect-free products. The rationale for empowering staff stems from the fact that often it is employees working lower down the organisational hierarchy that have the knowledge and understanding about how existing operational processes can be improved, but they often lack the power to make the necessary improvements. Empowering workers therefore often requires management to adjust their mindset and to view employees as a strategic asset and source of competitive advantage.

Achieving this change in the mindset of the management team at Grainger is likely to be relatively straightforward as empowerment is mentioned in the company's mission statement. Grainger could empower its staff further by giving them greater freedom to challenge management decisions and by also providing them with the resources and support needed to initiate and undertake employee-led work schemes. Such schemes could, for example, be directed at improving existing work processes or even developing new smartphones. Such schemes may enable Grainger to realise efficiencies in organisational processes or to make enhancements in the smartphones that it manufactures, thereby improving performance in the form of reduced costs and increased sales.

Empowering staff in this manner is likely to help Grainger to attract and retain the best people and therefore become an industry leading employer.

Engagement

For empowerment to be effective Grainger needs to ensure that its workers want to engage in the process of setting performance targets and improving performance. Grainger could look to enhance the process of engagement in a number of ways, including:

Establishing a talent management programme. Such schemes are concerned with attracting, identifying, developing, retaining individuals that are considered important to the organisation's future success. The introduction of such a scheme would be consistent with Grainger's existing approach to managing its human resources as the company's integrated report already outlines its commitment to attracting and retaining the best people. This is evident as staff already receive targeted training and a competitive employment package. The introduction of a talent management programme may help to make Grainger an even more appealing place to work as prospective employees may be attracted by the enhanced career prospects offered by such a scheme. As such, the process of staff engagement in performance improvement is likely to be enhanced if Grainger is viewed as being an employer of choice.

Set realistic targets and allow involvement. Setting realistic, relevant targets for individual employees, accompanied by a genuine desire among management to allow staff greater levels of involvement in determining their own performance targets may help Grainger achieve higher levels of employee engagement. For example, in the case of workers in Grainger's R&D department, realistic and relevant targets may relate to areas such as completing work on the latest smartphone prototypes by a given deadline or generating a predetermined number of new innovations for use in the company's smartphones over the course of a year. Due to the specialised nature of the work undertaken it may be appropriate to permit workers in the R&D team to have some input into how their performance will be measured, especially as the output from some of their innovations may not prove to be commercially viable at the current time but lead to viable outputs in the future.

Develop a culture and management style which embraces engagement. Grainger may be able to increase employee engagement in the process of performance management by developing a more open and transparent culture, which reinforces the aim of greater employee-manager collaboration. Employee engagement may be enhanced further by embracing the concept of distributive leadership, where work teams do not have an officially appointed leader. Such an approach may be highly appropriate at Grainger as many of the activities undertaken by the R&D and production teams are likely to have a greater focus on teamwork and problem-solving and will focus on implementing the ideas of the most knowledgeable specialist(s) as opposed to following the instructions of a single designated leader. The introduction of such an approach may facilitate a willingness among employees to get involved in the performance management process and the setting of team work targets.

Alignment

To achieve Grainger's vision 'to be recognised globally as the number one manufacturer of smartphones' the company will need to ensure that its corporate objectives are aligned to those of its workers and teams. This form of vertical alignment in Grainger's objectives is already evident to an extent as the company is likely to have corporate objectives relating to developing the latest smartphones, which are in turn supported by specific objectives for particular departments and individual workers. Workers in Grainger's R&D and production teams are likely to have individual objectives relating to maintaining their skills and industry knowledge in the field of smartphone development. This would appear likely given the fact that Grainger provides its staff with targeted training. Although, little is known in respect of Grainger's corporate objectives, the company should aim to enhance its performance further by ensuring that the objectives that its sets between departments and work teams are consistent, and not contradictory.

The horizontal alignment of these goals will be key in ensuring that the activities undertaken by the sales, R&D and production teams are consistent in the development and delivery of mobile phones that end users want.

Balanced scorecard – objectives and performance measures

Customer perspective

Objective

The introduction of G-3000 with its new battery and cutting-edge mobile phone technology represents an exciting new phase in the future of Grainger and therefore it is important that Grainger understands who the customers of the G-3000 will be, and the overall satisfaction levels that they will expect.

An appropriate objective for Grainger would be 'to satisfy the end user' and can be viewed from the perspective of both the retailers and the end-users of the G-3000.

Performance measure

An appropriate performance measure would be to measure the number of customer complaints received over a year. Such a measure could relate to the number of customer complaints received per 100 smartphones sold. This would provide a useful insight into customer satisfaction in respect of the performance of Grainger's products for both end users and retailers.

Grainger could use its customer surveys to measure customer satisfaction and to monitor the number of complaints it receives.

Innovation and learning perspective

Objective

To remain consistent with Grainger's objective to attract and retain the best people, the company should set an objective 'to create a challenging and interesting workplace' for all staff.

Performance measure

The performance measure here should be to keep staff turnover within a set percentage, for example less than 5% per annum of the total employees.

In light of its reliance on retaining key members of staff, minimising the costs associated with the recruitment and investment in training of new staff will be highly important to Grainger. As previously mentioned in sub-task (a), staff should be viewed as a source of competitive advantage for Grainger, with all reasonable steps being taken to maintain the best employees.

Internal business

Objective

As Grainger's staff have been thoroughly trained to produce defect-free products, it would be appropriate to formally set an objective which aims for zero defects in production.

Performance measure

While having an objective relating to zero defects in production is clearly appropriate, it is unlikely that this would be achievable 100% of the time given the number of things that could potentially go wrong in the production process. Nonetheless, such an objective could be measured by considering the percentage of defects in every 1,000 smartphone units produced.

This performance measure would involve regular inspection of samples of production with the aim of driving down the percentage of faulty units that are detected and rejected. Although the G-3000 smartphone is new, it is worth making the point that Grainger can take comfort from the fact that its internal processes must be working well, as the company has already been recognised as being one of the top three global mobile suppliers for product quality for each of the past 10 years.

TASK 6

Marking scheme — **Marks**

Sub-task (a): Autocratic leadership style at Diand — Up to 2 each

Up to 2 marks per relevant well-explained point which may include:

Appropriateness of an autocratic leadership style

- No one 'best style' of leadership
- Autocratic leadership has its limitations
- An autocratic approach is inconsistent with historic ways of working at Diand
- Leadership approach at Diand is indicative of a 'tells' style per Ashridge
- Assumption that workers dislike work and need constant supervision (Theory X)
- Not appropriate to the committed workers of Diand

Implications of autocratic leadership style

- Potential for high absenteeism and high staff turnover
- Potential for low morale and motivation – evident as new contract is behind schedule
- Failure to deliver contract would damage the reputation of the management team
- Uncertainty surrounding acquisition unlikely to have been addressed by the new leadership style

Recommendation to improve the current situation

- Adopt a 'consultative' leadership style
- Embrace McGregor's Theory Y approach
- Appropriate to committed attitude previously demonstrated by employees
- Likely to lead to greater job satisfaction and increased productivity

Maximum for sub-task (a) — **15**

Sub-task (b): Recognition of assets and liabilities; measurement issues Up to 2 each

Up to 2 marks per relevant well-explained point which may include:

IFRS 13 definition of fair value

Factory premises

- PPE should be recognised at its fair value
- IFRS 13 requires a market based measure so would use D$25m
- Not entity specific measure of D$23m

Brand name

- IAS 38 doesn't permit capitalisation of brand in individual accounts
- Recognised separately from goodwill (as intangible asset) when purchased as part of a business combination

Provision for training

- No obligation exists at acquisition so no provision for costs
- Recognise in post-acquisition period

Maximum for sub-task (b)	**10**
MAXIMUM FOR TASK 6	**25**

Suggested solution

Autocratic leadership style at Diand

Appropriateness of an autocratic leadership style

It is important to note that no one 'best' style of leadership exists, and very often the most appropriate style adopted will be driven by a range of factors, including the situation facing the leader and the capabilities and attitudes of those requiring leadership. In light of this, it is reasonable to accept that the autocratic approach does have its limitations.

Prior to the sale of Diand and appointment of the new management team, the workforce at Diand had historically enjoyed a strong relationship with the owners and managers of the company. This is evident as the loyalty of the workforce has, in the past, resulted in them stepping in to help to ensure the survival of the business, with workers taking pay cuts or agreeing to work longer hours.

The approach taken by the newly appointed management team at Diand would appear to be consistent with the 'tells' style proposed by the Ashridge Studies. The 'tells' style is classified as an autocratic leadership style. The 'tells' style involves the leader (or leaders) making all of the decisions affecting a team and then issuing instructions that must obeyed without question. This is evident at Diand as the new management team have simply told the workers of the changes in how their work is to be organised and have made it clear that there would be no room for discussion regarding how this would be achieved. The fact that the changes implemented by the new management team have resulted in changes to individual job roles and the breaking up of well-established teams so soon after Diand's acquisition by Grainger indicates that staff have not been permitted to contribute to these changes.

The imposition of disciplinary sanctions on those workers that have failed to comply with the new structure is consistent with McGregor's Theory X style. Theory X is based on the assumption that workers dislike and avoid work, are indifferent to the needs of the organisation and need constant supervision. The use of a Theory X approach would appear to be inconsistent with the situation at Diand especially in light of the commitment that its workers have historically displayed.

Implications of autocratic leadership style

In light of the situation described above, the use of an autocratic leadership style would already appear to be having a negative effect on Diand's workforce as this has not 'been well received'. This in turn may manifest itself in higher levels of absenteeism and potentially lead to an increase in staff turnover and lower levels of morale as staff gradually become disenchanted with the new management team. This may help to explain why production in respect of the new export contract has started to fall behind schedule.

Although, the new management team may be keen to enforce their authority over the workforce at Diand, this approach may prove to be counterproductive if workers refuse to step in and help to get the work back on schedule, as they would most likely have done in the past. A lack of willingness among the workforce due to perceptions about their treatment may potentially prove to be highly embarrassing for the new management team if Diand is unable to fulfil its commitments under the new export contract.

It is worth noting that the current unrest at Diand will most likely have been compounded by the uncertainty that would have resulted from the decision of Diand's original owners to sell the business in the first place.

Recommendation

The management team could look to diffuse the deteriorating situation at Diand by embracing a leadership style akin to a 'consultative' approach per the Ashridge studies. A consultative approach would involve the management team conferring with the workforce at Diand when making decisions that affect them, taking their views and concerns into account while retaining the final say on the end decision. Such an approach may help to create some 'buy in' among the workforce to the new management team's plans, thereby heightening feelings of motivation.

The consultative style would be more in line with McGregor's Theory Y approach which assumes workers are motivated by the enjoyment of their work and are prepared to work in order to meet organisational and personal goals. This style seems a better match to the committed attitude previously demonstrated by Diand's employees and is likely to lead to greater job satisfaction and increased levels of productivity.

Recognition of assets and liabilities; measurement issues

On acquisition of a subsidiary, IFRS 3 *Business Combinations* requires the subsidiary's assets and liabilities to be measured at fair value in the goodwill calculation. IFRS 13 *Fair Value Measurement* defines fair value as 'the price that would be received to sell an asset or paid to transfer a liability in an orderly transaction between market participants at the measurement date'. This definition has been applied to Diand's assets and liabilities below.

Factory premises

The property has already been correctly recognised in Diand's statement of financial position so it simply needs to be remeasured to its acquisition date fair value. As IFRS 13 requires use of a market-based measure, the market value of D$25 million is the most appropriate as it is the most objective. The D$23 million value is what we believe the asset to be worth to us and as such is an entity-specific measure and therefore, too subjective to use.

In the group accounts and in the goodwill calculation, we would need to increase the property from its carrying amount of D$20 million to its fair value of D$25 million.

Brand name

Under IAS 38 *Intangible Assets* internally generated brands may not be recognised as intangible assets because they cannot be distinguished from the business as a whole.

However, when they are acquired as part of a business combination (as they would be here when we purchase 100% of the equity shares of Diand), intangibles of the subsidiary should be recognised separately from goodwill irrespective of whether they had been recognised prior to the acquisition. The brand name would be included in the fair value of the net assets of Diand in the goodwill calculation and recognised as an intangible asset in the Grainger group accounts.

Provision for training

These training costs are an intention of Grainger at the acquisition date rather than an obligation. Therefore, they do not meet the *Conceptual Framework's* definition of a liability and under IFRS 3, should not be recognised as a liability on acquisition. Therefore, no provision would be included in the net assets of Diand in the goodwill calculation. Instead, any expense (and related provision) would be recognised when incurred in the post-acquisition period.

TASK 7

Marking scheme	**Marks**
Sub-task (a): Explanation of the use of activity-based costing at Grainger, including its benefits and limitations	Up to 2 each
Up to 2 marks per relevant well-explained point which could include:	
• What is activity-based costing?	
• Current approach to production overhead costs	
• Approach to production overhead using ABC	
• Benefits	
• Limitations	
• Impact on Grainger	
Maximum for sub-task (a)	**15**
Sub-task (b): Explanation of activity-based management and how it could be used by Grainger to improve performance	Up to 2 each
Up to 2 marks per relevant, well-explained point which could include:	
• What is activity-based management?	
• Analysis of activities	
• Product pricing	
• Design decisions	
• Quality assurance	
• Performance measurement	
Maximum for sub-task (b)	**10**
MAXIMUM FOR TASK 7	**25**

Suggested solution

Explanation of use of activity-based costing at Grainger, including its benefits and limitations

What is activity-based costing?

Activity-based costing (ABC) uses information on what creates overhead costs in Grainger's manufacturing processes (known as 'cost drivers'). It reflects the complexity and diversity of the modern manufacturing environment. ABC allocates those overheads to each mobile phone that is produced based on their consumption of the cost drivers. ABC gives a more realistic picture of overheads and this leads to better decisions on areas such as production numbers and selling prices.

Current approach to manufacturing overhead costs

The current approach at Grainger for allocating manufacturing overhead costs (whereby the total overhead cost is simply divided by production volumes to arrive at an overhead cost per unit) assumes that each mobile phone will consume each type of manufacturing overhead at the same rate.

Carla Letz is correct in her call for accurate cost data for each model of phone manufactured by Grainger so that her team feel that they are aiming for achievable budget targets. At the moment there is justification for the view that products are not being allocated their 'fair share' of costs, because the current approach to overhead allocation at Grainger is a simplistic one which ignores what drives overhead costs in the first place.

Approach to manufacturing overheads using ABC

Overhead costs at Grainger might include costs such as processing purchase orders for raw materials, machinery set up costs (likely to vary for each type of mobile phone), machinery maintenance and cleaning.

As an example, the total of a cost pool 'process purchase orders,' would be driven by the number of purchase orders processed on behalf of each product, while the total cost for the activity pool 'perform machinery set ups' would be driven by the number of set ups associated with each product. So, if a smartphone requires more machinery set up time than one of Grainger's basic mobile phones, smartphones should be allocated proportionately more of that particular overhead cost.

Benefits

ABC recognises the complexity of manufacturing businesses such as Grainger, with multiple cost drivers, many of which are based upon individual product features, rather than absolute production numbers in the manufacturing plant.

With a better understanding of costs and therefore margins, a more informed decision can be taken on whether to increase prices on certain ranges, in order to cover known costs and earn an acceptable margin. Grainger would, of course, need to consider whether its products will remain competitive at any revised prices.

Limitations

Although ABC leads to a more accurate way of relating overheads to our various phone models, it is not a perfect system, and will be based on a number of assumptions as to how costs are allocated. Detailed work will be needed to identify activities, cost pools and cost drivers, as the ABC system is further developed at Grainger, and management will need the help of all staff in undertaking this analysis.

Using ABC is not aimed at reducing costs. It can help Grainger to understand its costs better, but action would still have to be taken to improve or redesign activities in order to reduce costs (assuming that this is possible).

Impact on Grainger

The use of ABC at Grainger is still in very early stages of investigation, and if we extend it to examine all activities that make up our product costs, then the benefits for Grainger could be considerable in terms of cost understanding and management.

However, the amount of work in setting up an ABC system is considerable. From the sample cost card in Exhibit 1 only 4% of total costs relate to manufacturing labour and overheads. Grainger's management should therefore assess whether the cost of setting up such a system outweighs the benefits of having it before it is taken further.

How activity-based management could be used by Grainger to help improve performance

What is activity-based management?

Activity-based management (ABM) is a form of strategic cost management which seeks to identify and understand the activities that lead to product costs and aims to ensure both that these activities are performed efficiently, and that they add value for the organisation and its customers. ABM uses the information generated by ABC to control or reduce cost drivers and reduce overheads. By doing so, the company can gain competitive advantage.

Analysis of activities

An activity analysis will show the amount being spent on certain activities. Questions about the necessity for particular activities, and whether they can be carried out more efficiently, will help to focus management attention on processes that might not have been questioned before. For example, there are likely to be numerous quality checks at every stage of Grainger's production processes, which will involve significant cost, and might not all be necessary. Reducing or eliminating the need to perform some of these activities, especially if they do not add value for customers, could both reduce costs and lead to improvements in the service to Grainger's clients.

At a more ambitious level, strategic changes could be made to the way in which whole processes are undertaken (perhaps via outsourcing) if it is decided that the cost of in-house performance is too high. For example, it may be more cost effective and efficient to outsource the distribution function to a specialist fleet management company, which could further improve delivery times.

Product pricing

By accurately determining product costs, Grainger can then set prices for its ranges which achieve acceptable margins while remaining competitive. Given the fierce competition within the mobile phone industry, accurate product pricing is business critical for Grainger. At the strategic level, Grainger could use this accurate information to decide on new models or ranges to design and develop, or which products to discontinue. It could also help with alterations to the production mix, in favour of those ranges with higher margins, if ever there are capacity constraints.

Design decisions

ABM can help in making cost efficient decisions at the design stage. The way that a Grainger mobile phone is designed determines a large proportion of its eventual production costs, and these can be significantly reduced at the design stage, for example by reducing the number of different components and sub-assemblies required. This could include the use of standardised components, or a more limited range of raw materials.

Where decisions are being taken about new phone models, ABM can help in the assessment of the profitability of such developments by analysing the activities that are involved in their production. This could help avoid the development of unprofitable products.

Quality assurance

ABM also highlights the need for businesses to be focused on quality and continuous improvement. Grainger needs to be completely satisfied that its mission to provide quality mobile phones and exceed customer expectations in its design, delivery and cost continues to be supported. Quality inspection will always be required, both to comply with safety legislation and for commercial reasons, but Grainger could focus on quality initiatives aimed at getting its production processes 'right first time', perhaps helping to reduce the required number of checks as noted above.

Performance measurement

For ABM to be successful, it requires the commitment of senior management and effective communication and training of employees as to its benefits and methods. Continuous education and learning are core principles of Grainger.

New performance measurement systems will need to be developed. Employee rewards will need to be aligned to new measures, such as the reduction of non-value adding processes. This way, employees will be involved in Grainger's core business principle of maintaining focus upon quality design and production, and continuous improvement.

Task 8

Marking scheme	**Marks**
Sub-task (a): Key features of JIT, and how it could be used at Grainger Up to 2 marks per relevant well-explained point which could include: • Current inventory levels • JIT manufacturing • Manufacturing processes • JIT purchasing • Supply chain relationships • Staff involvement	Up to 2 each
Maximum for sub-task (a)	**15**
Sub-task (b): Explain TQM and its effects upon the costs of quality at Grainger Up to 2 marks per relevant, well-explained point which could include: • The concept of TQM • Right first time • Continuous improvement • Costs of quality • Some costs will initially increase • Commitment to quality	Up to 2 each
Maximum for sub-task (b)	**10**
MAXIMUM FOR TASK 8	**25**

Suggested solution

Key features of JIT, and how it could be used at Grainger

Current inventory levels

Grainger's inventory levels are high at 100 days or approximately 3.3 months. The inventory figure in the accounts is likely to comprise a buffer stock of popular mobile phones which are regularly ordered by customers, as well as raw materials and other components received from Grainger's network of suppliers. A significant amount of money is tied up within inventory (D$6,233 million at 20X5). Reducing inventory levels could release cash to be invested elsewhere within the business. Just-in-time (JIT) is a system whose objective is to produce products and obtain components only when they are required, rather than to hold them in inventory where they tie up working capital and incur handling and storage costs, and risk obsolescence, particularly with smartphones which are updated regularly.

JIT manufacturing

Grainger currently responds well to customer orders, with manufacturing starting as soon as confirmation of the order is received. With JIT production, the layout of Grainger's manufacturing plant should aim to minimise the movement of workers and products. Work flow is an important element in JIT, because the work needs to be completed without interruption in order to avoid a build-up of inventory.

Manufacturing processes

If it does not already do so, Grainger should group its machinery and workers by product, instead of by the type of work performed (assembly, testing etc). Products can then flow from machine to machine in their group, without having to wait for the next stage of processing. Lead times can be minimised, which will help Grainger achieve tight control of turnaround times and ensure delivery times meet customer expectations. With a streamlined flow of products through the manufacturing process, and direct delivery to customers, Grainger could grow its revenues as a result of even faster responses to customer demands.

JIT purchasing

JIT purchasing seeks to match the usage of materials with the delivery of materials from external suppliers. Grainger could benefit from JIT processes being applied to its inventory of regularly ordered phones, and its components of raw materials. This could mean that material inventories could be kept at near-zero levels. For JIT purchasing to be successful, Grainger must have confidence that its suppliers will continue to deliver quality materials and components on time, and that there will be no need for any returns or production delays. Usage of materials can be matched exactly with delivery of materials, and inventories can be kept at near zero levels.

Supply chain relationships

The reliability of suppliers is of critical importance, so relationships in the supply chain need to be strong. This could be achieved by doing more business with fewer suppliers. However, JIT will make Grainger far more vulnerable to disruptions in the supply chain, particularly with overseas suppliers where delivery lead times are lengthy. This may result in a need to source new suppliers locally.

Staff involvement

The ideal target through JIT is for Grainger to meet customer demand immediately, with perfect quality and no waste. In practice, this ideal is difficult to achieve. However, if Grainger is to work towards this ideal, JIT must be embraced by everyone, with training in JIT being another example of Grainger fulfilling one of its core business principles of being the industry-leading employer through its commitment to attract and retain the best people.

Explain Total Quality Management (TQM) and its effects upon the costs of quality at Grainger

The concept of TQM

TQM is an integrated and comprehensive system of planning and controlling all business functions so that products or services are produced which meet or exceed customer expectations. This is therefore extremely relevant to Grainger given that its mission is 'to provide high quality products and industry leading levels of customer service'. TQM can be implemented at Grainger by continually measuring performance levels achieved and aiming for continuous improvement in everything the company and its employees do.

Right first time

The key principle of TQM is 'get it right first time' – the belief that the costs of preventing mistakes in the first place are less than the costs of correcting these mistakes once they occur. For example, ensuring phones are manufactured correctly and tested before they are delivered to customers will reduce the number of phones returned under warranty due to manufacturing errors.

Continuous improvement

Another basic principle is dissatisfaction with the status quo – the belief that it is always possible to improve ('get it right next time'). This is known as continuous improvement. This will be a cultural change, from employees being used to working to achieve standard, to a new way of working where they are challenged to exceed standards. This achievement will then become the new standard to exceed.

Getting it right first time would mean introducing policies and procedures to ensure that errors in the manufacturing process do not occur. For example, an error in the manufacturing process resulting in a phone not being sealed correctly could lead to the corrosion of internal parts if the phone is exposed to water. Quality control over the manufacturing process should ensure this doesn't not happen. Continuous improvement, however, will go one step further and might also include the introduction of a new injection moulding technology being adapted to guarantee total water resistance of all phones manufactured by Grainger.

Costs of quality

There are four basic categories of costs of quality, divided into two types as follows:

Cost of compliance	Cost of failure
Prevention costs	Internal failure costs
Appraisal costs	External failure costs

Prevention costs are those costs incurred in trying to prevent any quality failures; such as the training of production staff and the maintenance of manufacturing equipment. Appraisal costs would include all inspection costs such as the use of quality control staff. Internal failure costs are the costs of correcting any issues before they reach the customer or an external party. So, if the quality control team found an error with a phone, it would be the cost of dealing with this– either scrapping the phone or re-working it. Finally, and this is the least desirable, is external failure costs. This is the cost of dealing with any quality issues which have already affected the customer. If there is an expense in this category, it suggests that all other stages have failed, and it can be very expensive to rectify reputation costs.

Some costs will initially increase

With the 'right first time' ethos of TQM, prevention costs should see an increase as there would be a lot of activity towards preventing failure eg quality circles to discuss each business area, creation of policies and procedures to ensure good quality and training of staff. However, this should have a positive effect on the other costs of quality. If Grainger do get it right, there should be no costs of failure at all. As costs of failure are usually disproportionate to what the costs would be to prevent failure, this should have a positive effect on the total costs of quality overall.

Over time, as the TQM initiative proves successful, it is also possible to reduce the costs of checking, since if you have all the processes in place to 'get it right' then the checking becomes redundant.

Commitment to quality

In order for TQM to work properly, everyone within Grainger must be committed to its principles and the ultimate objective of producing good quality mobile phones. In order to encourage this commitment, everyone would need to make suggestions that might improve quality, effectiveness or reduce costs for the same quality. In addition to this, the board will need to lead by example by ensuring that any worthwhile suggestions received from staff are actually considered.

TQM may cause concern and reduce motivation in employees because they may be worried that a focus on reducing costs may lead to staff redundancy. It will be important to effectively communicate the need for TQM and that by continuously improving the operations at Grainger there will be more job security as revenues grow and the business expands.

Recognising the importance of quality by accepting that the only thing that matters is the customer is therefore fundamental. Grainger should therefore focus everything on its customers' priorities.

Task 9

Marking scheme	**Marks**
Sub-task (a): Risks associated with each supplier	Up to 2 each
Up to 2 marks per relevant well-explained point which could include:	
Deeland Processors	
• Higher costs • Negotiating power • Lower returns for shareholders	
P-Tech	
• Unknown track record • Potential for supply delays • Foreign exchange risk • Political changes impacting supply	
Maximum for sub-task (a)	**12**
Sub-task (b): Practical considerations for negotiations	Up to 2 each
Up to 2 marks per relevant well-explained point which could include:	
• Culture/language • Location/currency • Testing • Price • Aftersales service • Establishing a good relationship	
Maximum for sub-task (b)	**13**
MAXIMUM FOR TASK 9	**25**

Tutorial note: You will earn marks for relevant points even if they are different from the ones we have included in the suggested solution.

Suggested solution

Risks associated with each supplier

Deeland Processors

Higher costs

Components purchased from Deeland Processors are expensive. As such Grainger will need to establish whether the high price offers good value for money in light of Deeland Processors' excellent reputation, or whether they charge inflated prices simply because they are known as being a premium supplier.

Negotiating power

Given Deeland Processors' strong market position they are unlikely to be flexible on price, meaning that Grainger risks not being able to benefit from any discounts.

Lower returns for shareholders

By paying too much for the processors Grainger runs the risk that returns to shareholders would be reduced. Here Grainger risks compromising return on capital if the purchase price of the processors is too high.

P-Tech

Unknown track record

As P-Tech are new to the Deeland market, their track record is unknown. There is a significant risk that the performance of their processors will be lower than Grainger currently obtains for similar components from existing suppliers. The concerns over P-Tech's working conditions that have been noted are also potentially alarming. These factors taken together could result in Grainger's costs being far higher than anticipated, especially if its own reputation is damaged by association.

Potential for supply delays

P-Tech are just starting to enter the Deeland market, and they may not have yet established a fully operational supply chain in Deeland. As such delivery lead times may be considerably longer than if Grainger were to purchase the processors that it needs from within Deeland. This represents a potentially significant risk as delays in receiving orders would impact on Grainger's own production processes when manufacturing the GR8.

Foreign exchange risk

There is an exchange risk attached to buying the processors from P-Tech. In the event the purchase price was stated in Zedland's currency, this would expose Grainger to exchange rate movements thereby potentially making the processors more expensive to buy than if they had been purchased from Deeland Processors. The risk here is that Grainger ends up paying more for what is potentially a lower quality product.

Political changes impacting supply

Zedland is a country that Grainger has no prior experience of dealing with. The fact that Zedland has experienced significant civil unrest in recent months represents a real concern. The ongoing situation coupled to any political changes that this might bring (eg a new government) could have a detrimental impact on Grainger's supply arrangements with P-Tech, especially if a new government introduced restrictions on exports to Deeland.

Practical considerations for negotiations

Culture and language

During the preparation stage of the negotiation process the negotiating team representing Grainger should give some consideration to the cultural and language factors which may have a bearing on the negotiation process. As Deeland Processors are based in Deeland there is unlikely to be any cultural or language issues to consider when negotiating with them. By contrast P-Tech are based in Zedland, and as such are likely to have a different national culture. As such representatives from Grainger should make initial contact with P-Tech to ascertain the extent of any cultural/language differences which may exist and factor this into the negotiation process.

Location/currency

As Grainger will be the customer regardless of which supplier is selected it seems reasonable to assume that both suppliers would want to make the effort to conduct the negotiations in Deeland. Conducting the negotiations in Deeland would help to communicate the seriousness of their interest in winning Grainger's business. With P-Tech being based in Zedland the negotiating team representing Grainger will need to confirm that the negotiations can be conducted in Deeland.

As part of these preparations the team should also ascertain whether Grainger could pay for the processors in D$ to avoid currency exchange costs.

Testing

Testing the processors offered by the two suppliers would form part of the opening stage in the negotiation process. Here the negotiating team at Grainger should test whether the processors offered by the two suppliers are in fact fit for purpose. Ideally this process should take place in Deeland when dealing with P-Tech as Grainger is the customer in this relationship. This process should help to identify any shortcomings in the two suppliers' offerings. Testing would most likely involve representatives from both Deeland Processors and P-Tech visiting Grainger's R&D department and presenting the capabilities of their processors. Representatives from Grainger may also want to visit both suppliers' production facilities in Deeland and Zedland respectively. This approach should provide some useful insight into whether the suppliers are likely to be capable of providing the quality and quantity of processors required. The findings from these tests and the site visits can then be used during the bargaining stage of the negotiations. The results during the testing phase may also provide Grainger with an option to get out of its supply arrangements should the quality of the processors supplied in the future fall.

Price

The negotiating team will need to be clear how much Grainger is prepared to spend when purchasing the processors. This needs to happen before negotiations begin and would form part of the preparation stage. It is likely that the negotiating team at Grainger would expect to pay more to purchase supplies from Deeland Processors as they are known to be a premium brand. Despite this the negotiating team may be able to negotiate a slightly lower price as Grainger has never purchased from Deeland Processors before, and as a result they may be willing to offer a better price to win Grainger's business. However, as highlighted in the solution to sub-task (a), there is no guarantee of this.

As P-Tech is already considered the cheaper option, the negotiating team representing Grainger may be able to negotiate even lower prices as it is known that P-Tech is keen to gain a presence in Deeland. Grainger will also need to specify what needs to be included within the purchase price for example, shipping costs. Price negotiations would form part of the opening and bargaining stage in the negotiation process.

Aftersales service

Component manufacturers often provide 'free' additional features such as warranties. If these are not included in the negotiated deal, then this could result in significant additional costs to Grainger should the processors fail to work properly. It is likely that the inclusion of warranties or assurances over the quality of the processors would form a standard part of any deal with Deeland Processors given the company's reputation.

Since P-Tech are new to the market and are based in another country the negotiating team at Grainger would need to ascertain whether these features are available as standard or not, and whether they are comparable to those offered by Deeland Processors. Gaining an understanding of such detail would most likely form part of the fact-finding stage during the preparation stage of the negotiation process.

Establishing a good relationship

Regardless of which supplier is chosen, if Grainger wants to do business with Deeland Processors or P-Tech in the future the negotiating team should seek to negotiate a deal that both parties are happy with. This is known as integrative bargaining, where the contracting parties aim for a win-win outcome. The negotiating team representing Grainger should not underestimate the importance of goodwill. Although getting the best possible deal is important, the establishment of a good relationship now could lead to even better deals in the future. Ensuring that both parties (regardless of which supplier is chosen) are happy with the negotiated deal would occur at the closing stage of the process.

Task 10

Marking scheme	**Marks**
Sub-task (a): Use of Big Data analytics capabilities to help Grainger improve its performance	Up to 2 each
Up to 2 marks per relevant well-explained point which could include: • Supply chain management • Product development • Correlation in sales trends • Decisions on the marketing mix • Analysing transactions	
Maximum for sub-task (a)	**10**
Sub-task (b): Practical implications of attempting to capture more end user data	Up to 2 each
Up to 2 marks per relevant well-explained point which could include: • Design, installation and maintenance costs • Political considerations • Data overload • Changing trends • Specialist skills • Data security • Time • Legal considerations	
Maximum for sub-task (b)	**15**
MAXIMUM FOR TASK 10	**25**

Tutorial note: You will earn marks for relevant points even if they are different from the ones we have included in the suggested solution.

Suggested solution

Use of Big Data analytics capabilities to help Grainger to improve its performance

Supply chain management

The successful use of Big Data analytics should enable Grainger to gain a better understanding of the attitudes and preferences of the end users that purchase its mobile phones from its customers (eg the network providers and independent retailers). Data could be captured from external sources and could include the internet searches made by end users looking for information about specific mobile phone models. Such data could be obtained from reputable internet search engines or social media networks. The possession of this kind of knowledge should enable Grainger to better manage its supply chain as it could identify those countries or regions where demand for particular models is highest. This would ensure that its most popular mobile phones are available for purchase in the right locations at the right time to meet the predicted demand among end users. This in turn should help to boost future sales performance.

Product development

The use of Big Data analytics could provide extremely useful feedback for future product development. For example, a series of posts left by end users on online forums may provide some insight into the mobile phone features that end users value as well as the features they would like to see when newer models are developed in the future. The use of Big Data analytics would build upon Grainger's current approach as it already obtains feedback on its products through the customer surveys that it uses. The use of Big Data analytics capabilities should help Grainger to make improved product mix decisions which should help to grow the company's revenue.

Correlation in sales trends

Between 20X4 and 20X5 Grainger achieved a positive increase in its sales as these rose by 13.8%. Although, Grainger will have access to its own internal sales data showing the number of mobile phones sold and the types of models sold, the company may not necessarily fully understand the correlation between the sales made and other underlying external factors that may have contributed to these sales. This is where the use of Big Data analytics might be able to help. For example, Grainger may be able to capture external data that shows the state of the economy in specific countries. It may be the case that in some instances Grainger may identify that an improvement in the state of the economy led to end users in that country having a higher level of disposable income, which in turn translated into greater volumes of sales. A better understanding of the correlation between sales and external events should help Grainger to plan its production activities more effectively and may enable the company to reduce its costs and the size of its production runs if reduced demand in certain countries can more effectively be predicted. The reverse may also be true in cases where production can be increased to capitalise on opportunities in certain markets.

Decisions on the marketing mix

Big Data analytics tools could also be used to improve strategic decision making at Grainger. Instant feedback on social media regarding Grainger's range of mobile phones could be used to inform elements of the company's marketing mix. For example, if a model of mobile phone was found to not be selling well in a country, data from end user feedback (perhaps regarding its price, packaging, selling channels or the promotions used) could be used to make decisions about distribution and pricing policies in that country.

Analysing transactions

Grainger may be able use Big Data analytics software to analyse transactional sales data captured by its network provider and independent retailer customers regarding all of the mobile phones that they sell, regardless whether they are manufactured by Grainger or not. Clearly, this approach would only be viable if Grainger's customers agree to collaborate and share their own internal data. Such data may provide Grainger with useful insights into the types of purchases that end users of mobile phones are making. This may help Grainger to assess both the frequency of purchase and gain a better understanding of the most popular mobile phones made by other manufacturers. Again, such data could be used to identify trends in purchasing behaviours (preferences and spending habits by geographical region, for example) and would allow Grainger to gauge potential future moves by competitors in terms of the types of mobile device that they may develop in the future. The ability to pre-empt opposing moves by competitors should help Grainger to develop more effective strategies to ensure that its own performance is not detrimentally impacted.

Practical implications of attempting to capture more end user data

Design, installation and maintenance costs

Capturing more data about end users would most likely require Grainger to make improvements to its existing IT infrastructure. The associated costs are likely to be significant. Building an IT infrastructure capable of storing and interrogating Big Data drawn from a variety of sources, including social media posts about the latest mobile phone technologies, may prove prohibitively expensive.

Political considerations

An attempt to capture more data about end users through enhancing Grainger's IT infrastructure might cause political conflict at board level. Trying to convince the board that capturing more data as part of Grainger's sales and marketing activity could be perceived as conflicting with the strategic decision in 20X2 to downsize the sales department. Furthermore, Frank Williams's assertion that CEO, Nisha Patel, has become increasingly complacent towards the work for the sales department, coupled with an attempt to increase the department's remit, may be perceived as a challenge to her leadership and may cause conflict.

Data overload

Consideration needs to be given to which end user data sets are likely to be of use to Grainger. There is an inherent danger with all data collection that too much of the wrong type of data is captured. This often occurs when the needs of the business are not determined in advance. Data which fails to inform management decisions, or focuses for example on pursuing low value end users, such as those who purchase pay as you go phones, can be regarded as the wrong data.

Changing trends

Careful consideration needs to be given to the fact that end users that purchase their phones from network providers on two-year contracts will most likely change their model of phone at the end of their contract term. The short lifecycle of mobile phone contracts increases the chance that by the time Grainger has captured data about end user preferences, that the company may not have enough time to integrate the findings from this data (eg the mobile phone features that customers now expect) into the next generation of smartphone that the customer purchases.

Specialist skills

Consideration needs to be given to whether Grainger's sales department have the required skills to be able to extract meaningful insights from the data they capture. Given the decision to reduce the size of the market research team in 20X2 it is unlikely that any of the existing employees in the sales department will have experience in analysing large data sets. This supports Frank William's desire to establish a dedicated data analytics team which would possess the required skills. This option has significant cost implications.

Data security

The board at Grainger will need to ensure that adequate measures are put in place to stop end user data being accessed by hackers. Working closely with a reliable IT services company should help address some of these concerns.

Time

Capturing end user data is likely to consume a significant amount of Grainger's management's time in determining the types of data to be captured. Furthermore, if capturing end user data is to be facilitated by upgrading Grainger's existing IT infrastructure then consideration will need to be given to any potential disruption that this may cause Grainger's existing IT systems in terms of potential downtime.

Legal considerations

Consideration needs to be given to the legal factors associated with capturing end user data. As Grainger is a global manufacturer with its mobile phones available in most countries it is likely that different countries will have their own laws in place to protect the personal data of individuals. Grainger will need to be mindful of this to ensure that it does not contravene relevant laws in certain jurisdictions.

Task 11

Marking scheme **Marks**

Sub-task (a): Analysis of financial performance Up to 2 each

Up to 2 marks per relevant well-explained point which could include:

Gross margin

- Stable year on year
- Expansion (mainly in Middle East and Europe)
- Despite expansion, no apparent bulk buy discounts/economies of scale

Operating margin

- Improved despite stable gross margin
- Improvement in non-production overheads cost control
- Increases in operating margin of Europe, Asia, America and other regions
- Largest growth in only region with falling margin (Middle East): unstable political climate
- Strong growth in Europe – good strategy as region with highest margin

Return on capital employed

- Improved due to increase in operating margin
- Despite new loans taken out in year/investments in non-current assets

Conclusion

- Improved financial performance from 20X4 to 20X5

Maximum for sub-task (a) **15**

Sub-task (b): Possible actions to improve financial performance Up to 2 each

Up to 2 marks per relevant well-explained point which could include:

- Negotiate with suppliers
- Product development
- Staff motivation
- Reduction in overheads
- Geographical coverage

Maximum for sub-task (b) **10**

MAXIMUM FOR TASK 11 **25**

Tutorial note: You will earn marks for **relevant** points even if they are different from the ones we have included in the suggested solution.

For sub-task (a), no calculations are required, and no marks will be awarded for calculations. However, you can include simple percentage increases and decreases in order to illustrate your points.

A point that simply states whether a ratio has increased or decreased in the year will not be awarded two marks. To achieve two marks, your answer must explain the reason **why** the ratios differ, linking the ratios to the financial statements and narrative information from the abridged pre-seen to assist you.

For sub-task (b), there are many possible valid points which will be given credit as long as they are commercially viable and properly applied to Grainger.

Suggested solution

Analysis of financial performance

Gross margin

Grainger's gross margin has remained stable year on year, demonstrating consistency in the operation of our core activities.

Even though Grainger has expanded during the year with a 14% growth in revenue, cost of sales as also increased by 14%. Therefore, we do not appear to have benefited from any bulk buy discounts of parts or economies of scale as a result of the expansion.

The biggest growth has been in the Middle East (57% increase in revenue) and Europe (26% increase in revenue).

Operating margin

Grainger's operating margin has improved despite the gross margin remaining constant. This is because despite a 14% increase in revenue and cost of sales, research and development expenses and selling and administrative expenses have only increased by 1% and 2% respectively. This indicates good cost control of non-production overheads. However, in such a fast-moving technological industry as mobile phones, we do need to ensure that we are investing sufficiently in research and development. It is encouraging to see new development costs of D$30 million in the year.

The increase in our operating margin can be largely attributed to strong increases in profit across four of our five geographical regions (Europe, Asia, America and Other). It is slightly worrying though that the region that has grown most in the year (Middle East with a 57% increase in revenue) has an operating margin that fell from 12% in 20X4 to 10% in 20X5. The civil unrest and the political climate in this region are likely to have played a part in this decline. The increase in revenue could also be driven by a decrease in selling price resulting in lower margins.

Whilst we might be reaching market saturation in Asia (a 1% increase in revenue), it is encouraging to see the growth potential in both the Middle East and Europe. The 26% increase in European revenue year on year demonstrates effective management strategy as it is one of the regions with the highest operating margin (14%).

Return on capital employed (ROCE)

Grainger's ROCE has improved year on year. This is largely due to the increase in the operating margin.

The improvement is impressive given that we would expect the new loans taken out in the year and the investment in non-current assets to cause a decrease in ROCE.

Conclusion

Grainger is successfully achieving a strategy of expansion with continuous annual increases in the number of mobile phones since 20X0. At the same time, Grainger has improved its financial performance through growth in its operating margin and an increase in its return on capital employed.

Possible actions to improve financial performance

Negotiate with suppliers

Grainger should continue to build on its relationships with suppliers, treating them as part of the organisational ecosystem. This should include continuing to invest in joint projects with suppliers. A strong relationship with suppliers combined with Grainger's continued expansion should help Grainger to negotiate bulk buy discounts for parts which will help improve the gross margin going forward.

Product development

Grainger should continue to invest in research and development in order to exploit opportunities offered by new improved versions of operating systems and new apps when improving its range of 4G phones. Further opportunities exist, including flexible foldable phones, waterproof phones and convenient charging methods.

It should also continue to investigate the potential of 5G as in the longer term, as this should give Grainger access to new products both in the form of improved smartphones and the 'internet of things' (eg wearable devices).

If Grainger succeeds in bringing these new innovative products to market before its competitors, it will be able to charge premium prices and achieve a high margin, which will improve its financial performance.

Staff motivation

Grainger is committed to attracting and retaining the best people. Its policies include targeting training, additional leave for charitable courses and competitive remuneration. Going forward, Grainger should continue with this approach and consider tailoring its training to specifically target staff efficiency, particularly in the case of manufacturing workers in its factories. For example, measures could be introduced to increase the output of phones and to reduce wastage.

Performance-related remuneration for factory workers could be directly linked to output by employee or innovative suggestions. Grainger could also introduce awards for 'employee of the month' or 'team of the month'. The more valued the employees feel, the more motivated they are likely to be which should help to optimise their performance.

Reduction in overheads

Grainger could make savings in overheads by establishing a team in the finance department to investigate potential alternative suppliers and better deals for utilities such as electricity, gas, water, phone and internet services. It may also be possible to find cheaper insurance cover and a cheaper supplier of office supplies and equipment.

Geographical coverage

Grainger should continue to pursue a policy of expansion in Europe and Asia which are its two biggest markets and the markets with the highest operating margin (14%). Continued growth here will help increase the company's overall margin.

However, Grainger needs to investigate the reason for the decline in operating margin of its most rapidly growing region, the Middle East. A project team could be established to try to identify possible ways of improving the margin in the Middle East.

Although Grainger is a global manufacturer with products available in most countries, there are still some countries where the products are not yet available. The sales team could be targeted with investigating possible new markets or moving manufacturing to countries with lower labour costs.

TASK 12

Marking scheme	Marks
Sub-task (a): Managing the conflict	Up to 2 each
Up to 2 marks per relevant well-explained point which could include:	
• Thomas and Kilmann's conflict-handling strategies	
• Grainger versus former DGP workers	
• Disruptive behaviour	
• Options for managing the conflict	
• Collaboration = recommended approach	
• Consideration of other factors eg change issues	
• Discuss with Thomas Allen	
• Need to uphold ethical standards	
Maximum for sub-task (a)	**15**
Sub-task (b): Appropriateness of Sales Director's suggestion	
Up to 2 marks per relevant well-explained point which could include:	Up to 2 each
• Proposed an avoidance strategy	
• Removes the need for immediate action/ 'brush it under the carpet'	
• Results in further disruption for other workers and managers	
• Could lead to production ceasing altogether	
• May result in other Grainger workers become demotivated	
• Sales Director's strategy is inappropriate	
Maximum for sub-task (b)	**10**
MAXIMUM FOR TASK 12	**25**

> **Tutorial note:** You will earn marks for relevant points even if they are different from the ones we have included in the suggested solution.

Suggested solution

Managing the conflict

Thomas and Kilmann's conflict-handling strategies

Thomas and Kilmann proposed five conflict-handling strategies that organisations can use when seeking to address conflict. Thomas and Kilmann suggest that conflict-handling strategies can be mapped on two dimensions, according to the intentions of the parties involved: assertiveness (which is concerned with trying to satisfy one's own concerns) and cooperativeness (trying to satisfy the other party's concerns).

Grainger versus former DGP workers

The parties in conflict at Grainger are the workers that were formerly employed by DGP and those workers and managers that were employed in Grainger's production team prior to the DGP acquisition. The intention of the former DGP workers would appear to be focused on re-creating the culture that existed in the production department at DCP before the acquisition. This is supported by the remark made by one of the former DGP workers that Carla Letz overheard and the fact that members of this group are unwilling to adjust to Grainger's ways of working.

This issue would appear to have been compounded by the changes made to this group's contracts of employment which now require them to work an extra hour per day. Although, not an unreasonable course of action, especially as Grainger has increased this group's salary to bring them in line with its existing production workers, it would appear that this change has only further highlighted the differences between working at DGP and Grainger.

Disruptive behaviour

Deliberate failure to undertake the charity work, withholding information and disobeying instructions are disruptive behaviours that are affecting the harmony of the entire production team as this has resulted in a lack of cooperation between the two groups and which has been characterised as bordering on hostile.

Options for managing the conflict

To address the current situation the board at Grainger should look to make use of Thomas and Kilmann's conflict-handling strategies which consist of the following:

Avoidance – Grainger could seek to avoid, suppress or ignore the conflict.

Accommodation – Grainger could aim to put the DGP workers' interests first and suppress their own interests in order to preserve some form of stability with a view to suppressing the conflict.

Compromise – Grainger could aim to reach a negotiated agreement on addressing the conflict with the DGP workers. This would, however, require both parties losing something.

Competition/forcing – Grainger and the DGP workers could decide to not cooperate, and instead seek to maximise their own interests and goals, thereby resulting in a win-lose scenario for one of the parties.

Collaboration – This strategy would involve Grainger and the DGP workers confronting their differences and jointly resolving any issues with the aim that a win-win outcome is achieved.

On the face of it, the behaviour of the former DGP workers, which is largely unprofessional, may appear to warrant adopting a competition/forcing conflict-handling style which would result in one party losing (eg the former DGP workers) and the other party (Grainger) winning. This could be achieved by Grainger seeking to impose disciplinary sanctions on this group in response to their unprofessional behaviour.

Collaborative approach

Alternatively, the board at Grainger could look to pursue a collaborative approach. Pursuing a competition/forcing approach heightens the risk of the former DGP workers opting to leave Grainger (provided they are not dismissed for gross misconduct), thereby seriously undermining the reason that Grainger acquired DGP in the first place. This is supported by the fact that Grainger had sought to acquire DGP for a long time as it was keen to gain access to those production and R&D professionals with specialist expertise in the field of smartphone screen manufacture.

Consideration of other factors

As the former DGP workers are professionals in their field, this increases the appropriateness of adopting a collaborative approach as they may be prepared to work with the board at Grainger to address the underlying issues which have given rise to their behaviours with a view to developing a new relationship with their employer.

Although it does excuse their disruptive behaviours, it is worth noting that the former DGP workers have endured a significant amount of upheaval in recent months, especially given that the acquisition by Grainger only took place six months ago. The uncertainty and change associated with the acquisition may have contributed to rational professionals behaving in a disruptive manner and may also raise some questions about how Grainger managed the acquisition from a change management perspective.

Discussion with Thomas Allen

As Grainger also retained the services of workers from DGP's R&D team following the acquisition, it would be worth Carla Letz discussing the current situation with Thomas Allen, Grainger's Head of R&D, to ascertain whether he had experienced any similar issues with former DGP workers.

Need to uphold ethical standards

Regardless of the conflict-handling strategy adopted the board at Grainger need to ensure that they uphold the ethical standards of integrity and professionalism.

Appropriateness of the Sales Director's suggestion

Proposed an avoidance strategy

Frank William's suggestion of ignoring the conflict is effectively the same as Thomas and Kilmann's avoidance conflict-handling strategy, whereby one party (which in this case would be the board at Grainger) effectively avoids the conflict by refusing to deal with it.

Removes the need for immediate action/'brush it under the carpet'

This approach would remove the immediate need for the board at Grainger to do anything. However, viewing the current situation as a temporary issue is tantamount to 'brushing it under the carpet'.

Results in further disruption for other workers and managers

However, this 'brush it under the carpet approach' is likely to result in the other workers and managers in Grainger's production team encountering further disruption from the former DGP workers. The current behaviours of the former DGP workers are only likely to worsen until the situation is dealt with.

Could lead to production ceasing altogether

Over time, further disruptive behaviours may cause Grainger's production operations to completely cease if the two groups are unable to work together. Such an event could have a devastating impact on Grainger's entire operations and may even threaten the survival of the company.

May result in other Grainger workers becoming demotivated

It is also worth noting that by ignoring the current situation, this may upset and demotivate the other workers and managers employed in Grainger's production team. This group may experience feelings of having been neglected by the board as they would still experience the ongoing issues that are currently being caused by the other group.

Sales Director's strategy is inappropriate

As the former DGP workers are paid employees of Grainger, it is not unreasonable to expect them to follow reasonable instructions issued by managers in the production team, nor is it unreasonable to expect them to share work-related information with their colleagues, regardless of how they view the acquisition of DGP. As such Frank William's approach is not an appropriate way of handling the matter.

Tell us what you think

Got comments or feedback on this book? Let us know.
Use your QR code reader:

Or, visit:
https://www.smartsurvey.co.uk/s/BAJPTT/

Need to get in touch with customer service?

www.bpp.com/request-support

Spotted an error?

https://learningmedia.bpp.com/pages/errata